Betty Crocker

Sheet Pan Desserts

Delicious Treats You Can Make with a Sheet, 13x9 or Jelly Roll Pan

Houghton Mifflin Harcourt

Boston · New York

GENERAL MILLS

Owned Media and Publishing Director:
Amy Halford

Owned Media and Publishing Manager:
Audra Carson

Senior Editor: Cathy Swanson

Recipe Development and Testing:
Betty Crocker Kitchens

Photography: General Mills Photography
Studios and Image Library

HOUGHTON MIFFLIN HARCOURT

Publisher: Natalie Chapman

Editorial Director: Cindy Kitchel

Executive Editor: Anne Ficklen

Editorial Associate: Molly Aronica

Managing Editor: Marina Padakis

Production Editor: Helen Seachrist

Cover Design: Tai Blanche

Interior Design and Layout: Tai Blanche

Senior Production Coordinator:
Kimberly Kiefer

Library of Congress Cataloging-in-Publication Data is available.

ISBN 978-0-544-81623-7 (trade paper); ISBN 978-0-544-81626-8 (ebk)

Manufactured in the U.S.A.

DOC 10 9 8 7 6 5 4 3 2

4500635154

Cover photo: Peanut Butter–Chocolate–Toffee Crunch, page 256

The Betty Crocker Kitchens seal guarantees
success in your kitchen. Every recipe has been
tested in America's Most Trusted Kitchens™
to meet our high standards of reliability, easy
preparation and great taste.

FIND MORE GREAT IDEAS AT
BettyCrocker.com

Dear Bakers,

What's a Sheet Pan Dessert? It's a delicious treat for a crowd that you bake in only one batch! Think simple, delicious and smart. Baking desserts in your bigger pans—jelly roll (cookie sheet with sides), 13x9-inch pans and on cookie sheets—is a great way to save time in the kitchen.

In *Betty Crocker Sheet Pan Desserts,* you'll find cool, make-ahead refrigerator and frozen desserts perfect for a hot summer gathering or when hosting a girl's night. Our sheet cakes and one-layer cakes are perfect for potlucks or grad parties—both easy to tote and serve. Browse through all of the brownie, bar and cookie bar recipes when you are asked to bring something to share or have a lot of cookie thieves in the house! We've even got amazing slab pies that offer the perfect ratio of filling to crust—you may never make a round pie again.

But that's not all. Our "Hosting a Bake Sale" feature will show you exactly how to pull off a successful homemade treat fund-raiser and have a ball doing it. We'll show you how to cut bars in fun, exciting shapes—no more squares! And we'll show you irresistible ways to turn brownies into show-stopping desserts like brownie shooters, ice-cream sandwiches or shortcake. From cookie jar sweets to indulgent, make-ahead desserts, whether hosting a big bash, going to a potluck or wanting to have enough homemade goodies that will last more than a day before getting eaten, you'll find the perfect recipe here.

Bake on, bake proud!
Betty Crocker

Look for these helpful icons throughout the book. The 15 minute prep icon means 15 minutes of prep time or less.

JELLY ROLL PAN	13 × 9	COOKIE SHEET
15 MIN. PREP	NO BAKE	STARTS WITH A MIX
	HOMEMADE MIX	

CONTENTS

Introduction 6

Sheet Pan Desserts

What is a sheet pan dessert? Basically, it's a dessert made in one pan that serves a lot of people. It's a perfect solution when feeding a crowd or taking a dish to a potluck. Many of these desserts can be made ahead, taking the stress out of entertaining. There's no fussing over a dessert when the guests are there—it's already made and ready to serve when you are!

What Is a Sheet Pan?

Sheet pans can mean different things to different people. Traditionally, a sheet pan (or jelly roll pan) is what many refer to as a cookie sheet with sides. It's usually 15x10x1 inch. But the term has been broadened to include other pans that make a large batch at one time. This book contains recipes made in jelly roll, 13x9 pans and on cookie sheets.

Choosing Pans

Having the right pan can mean the difference between chewy textured bars or bars with dry, over-baked edges. If the dessert isn't being baked, the pan material isn't as critical. For the majority of recipes where baking is required, here's what we recommend no matter what type of sheet pan you are using:

- **SHINY ALUMINUM WITH SMOOTH SURFACE** The top choice for baking desserts, as the shiny surface reflects the heat, allowing for even baking and browning.
- **NONSTICK AND DARK-SURFACE** Desserts baked in these pans may result in darker tops, edges and especially the bottoms. Follow the manufacturer's directions as many have you reduce the oven temperature by 25°F. Check desserts at minimum time so they don't get too brown.
- **INSULATED COOKIE SHEETS** These sheets help from becoming too dark on the bottom so additional bake time may be needed. It may be more difficult to remove desserts baked on these sheets, as the bottoms could be more tender.

To Grease or Not to Grease

If a recipe calls for greasing the pan, use either cooking spray or shortening. Lining the pan with foil is an easy way to remove desserts such as brownies or bars for ease in cutting and pan clean-up. Foil is great for either pans with sides or flat cookie sheets. Parchment paper is also great for cookie sheets and can be used with pans with sides but is a little more difficult to work with because it doesn't hold its shape as easily. If you find rolls of parchment hard to work with, as pieces keep rolling up when you try to flatten them, look for flat sheets of parchment, available from cake supply or craft stores.

Lining the Pan with Foil

Turn the pan upside down and cut the foil 4 inches larger than the pan. Form foil over the pan bottom and sides. Lift foil off pan and flip pan right-side up. Place the shaped foil inside the pan. When the bars or brownies have cooled, lift them from the pan using the overhanging foil edges; peel back the foil to cut the bars.

Cutting Beautiful Pieces

A dessert may look beautiful in the pan, but how do you get beautiful pieces onto serving plates? Picking the right tool for the job (and knowing a few insider tricks of the trade) will help serve up show-stopping desserts.

- **SHARP KNIFE** Choose knives with a sharp tip and a wide enough blade for cutting through desserts with one motion or as few as possible. Serrated knives work well when there are pieces of nuts or chips in the dessert that need to be cut through. Straight-bladed knives are great for smooth-textured desserts.

- **PLASTIC KNIFE** Those picnic-worthy flatware knives are actually the perfect tool for cutting brownies and other fudgy-type bars. The plastic surface helps to cut through them cleanly, leaving nicely shaped sides.

- **WET KNIFE** Use a sharp knife that's been dipped in water to cut through sticky or soft desserts. The trick is to have the knife be a little wet but not dripping so that the water isn't transferred to the dessert, making it soggy in spots. Repeat this process after one or up to several cuts as need.

- **KNIFE SPRAYED WITH COOKING SPRAY** Spraying a knife with cooking spray is sometimes useful when desserts are particularly sticky. It helps prevent the sticky mixture from clinging to the knife, making it drag through the dessert instead of cutting cleanly.

CHOOSE THE RIGHT SERVER It's always best to choose a big enough server that will cover as much of the surface area of the bottom of the dessert as possible—but not too big. The right size server can lift the piece easily to the serving plate without any of the piece falling off. If the server is too large, it can damage the pieces around it in the pan as you lift out the piece you are serving. Servers are usually thinner than spatulas, making it easier to get under a serving to help get it to the plate in a pretty shape. Having a variety of sizes and shapes of servers in your kitchen will help you have the right tool for the job.

Kitchen Tools

cooling rack

oven mitt

cookie sheet

15 × 10 × 1 jelly roll pan

13 × 9 sheet pan

serving spatula

whisk

liquid
measuring cup

parchment
paper sheet

knife

metal spatula

dry measuring cup and spoons

dry measuring cups

measuring
spoons

parchment
paper roll

kitchen
towel

aluminum
foil

CHAPTER ONE

Refrigerated and Frozen Desserts

Luscious Key Lime Dessert

20 servings | Prep Time: 15 Minutes | Start to Finish: 1 Hour 30 Minutes

1 pouch (1 lb 1.5 oz) oatmeal cookie mix

½ cup cold butter

2 cans (14 oz each) sweetened condensed milk (not evaporated)

¾ cup Key lime juice or lime juice

1 container (16 oz) frozen whipped topping, thawed

2 containers (6 oz each) Key lime pie fat-free yogurt

Few drops green food color, if desired

1 tablespoon grated lime peel

½ cup fresh berries (blueberries, raspberries, strawberries)

1 Heat oven to 350°F. Spray bottom and sides of 13x9-inch pan with cooking spray.

2 Place cookie mix in large bowl. Cut in butter, using pastry blender or fork, until mixture is crumbly and coarse. Lightly press crumbs in bottom of pan. Bake 10 to 12 minutes or until golden brown. Cool.

3 In large bowl, beat condensed milk and lime juice with electric mixer on medium speed until smooth and thickened. Reserve 1 cup of the whipped topping; refrigerate until serving time. Fold remaining whipped topping, the yogurt and food color into milk mixture. Spoon into cooled baked crust. Cover; refrigerate about 1 hour or until set.

4 Cut into 5 rows by 4 rows. Garnish each serving with a dollop of reserved whipped topping, lime peel and berries. Store covered in refrigerator.

1 Serving: Calories 340; Total Fat 13g (Saturated Fat 9g, Trans Fat 0g); Cholesterol 25mg; Sodium 190mg; Total Carbohydrate 50g (Dietary Fiber 0g); Protein 6g
Exchanges: ½ Starch, 2 Other Carbohydrate, 1 Milk, 1 Fat **Carbohydrate Choices:** 3

Strawberries and Cream Squares

20 squares | Prep Time: 30 Minutes | Start to Finish: 2 Hours 30 Minutes

CRUST

- 1 pouch (1 lb 1.5 oz) sugar cookie mix
- ½ cup butter, softened
- 1 egg

FILLING

- 1 cup white vanilla baking chips
- 1 package (8 oz) cream cheese, softened

TOPPING

- 4 cups sliced fresh strawberries
- ½ cup sugar
- 2 tablespoons cornstarch
- ⅓ cup water
- 10 to 12 drops red food color, if desired

1. Heat oven to 350°F. Spray bottom only of 15x10x1-inch jelly roll pan with cooking spray.

2. In large bowl, stir crust ingredients until soft dough forms. Press mixture in bottom of pan.

3. Bake 15 to 20 minutes or until light golden brown. Cool completely in pan on cooling rack, about 30 minutes.

4. In small microwavable bowl, microwave baking chips uncovered on High 45 to 60 seconds or until chips are melted and can be stirred smooth. In medium bowl, beat cream cheese with electric mixer on medium speed until smooth. Stir in melted chips until blended. Spread mixture over crust. Refrigerate while making topping.

5. In small bowl, crush 1 cup of the strawberries. In 2-quart saucepan, mix sugar and cornstarch. Stir in water and crushed strawberries. Cook and stir over medium heat until mixture boils and thickens. Remove from heat; stir in food color. Cool 10 minutes.

6. Gently stir in remaining 3 cups strawberries. Spoon over filling. Refrigerate 1 hour or until set but no longer than 4 hours. Cut into 5 rows by 4 rows.

1 Square: Calories 270; Total Fat 13g (Saturated Fat 8g, Trans Fat 1g); Cholesterol 35mg; Sodium 150mg; Total Carbohydrate 34g (Dietary Fiber 0g); Protein 3g **Exchanges:** 1 Starch, 1 Other Carbohydrate, 2½ Fat **Carbohydrate Choices:** 2

The Wow Factor For a decadent garnish, make Sweetened Whipped Cream (page 109), to dollop on squares; drizzle lightly with chocolate syrup.

Easy Strawberry-Cream Dessert Squares

18 squares | Prep Time: 25 Minutes | Start to Finish: 4 Hours

1 roll (16.5 oz) refrigerated sugar cookies

2 packages (8 oz each) cream cheese, softened

¼ cup sugar

1 cup strawberry topping (from 11.75-oz jar)

2 eggs

1 container (16 oz) frozen whipped topping, thawed

4 to 6 drops red food color

Fresh strawberries, if desired

1 Heat oven to 350°F. Press cookie dough in bottom of ungreased 13x9-inch pan. (If dough is sticky, use floured fingers.)

2 In medium bowl, beat cream cheese, sugar and ¾ cup of the strawberry topping with electric mixer on medium-high speed about 1 minute or until well blended. Add eggs; beat about 2 minutes or until well blended and creamy. Spread evenly over crust.

3 Bake 30 to 35 minutes or until center is set. Cool in pan on cooling rack 1 hour. Center will sink slightly as it cools.

4 In medium bowl, mix whipped topping, food color and remaining ¼ cup strawberry topping. Spread over cream cheese layer. Refrigerate about 2 hours or until set. Cut into 6 rows by 3 rows. Garnish with strawberries. Store covered in refrigerator.

1 Square: Calories 340; Total Fat 18g (Saturated Fat 10g, Trans Fat 1.5g); Cholesterol 55mg; Sodium 180mg; Total Carbohydrate 39g (Dietary Fiber 0g); Protein 3g **Exchanges:** 1 Starch, 1½ Other Carbohydrate, 3½ Fat **Carbohydrate Choices:** 2½

Gluten-Free Easy Fruit Pizza

24 servings | Prep Time: 20 Minutes | Start to Finish: 2 Hours 10 Minutes

1   box (15 oz) gluten-free sugar cookie mix

1   egg

¼   cup butter, softened

3   tablespoons canola or vegetable oil

1½ teaspoons gluten-free vanilla

1   package (8 oz) ⅓-less-fat cream cheese (Neufchâtel), softened

⅓   cup sugar

2   kiwifruit, peeled, halved lengthwise and sliced

1   cup halved or quartered fresh strawberries

1   cup fresh blueberries

¼   cup apple jelly

1 Heat oven to 350°F. Line 15x10x1-inch jelly roll pan with cooking parchment paper; spray paper with cooking spray (without flour).

2 In large bowl, stir cookie mix, egg, butter, oil and 1 teaspoon of the vanilla until dough forms. Break up dough in pan; press evenly in bottom of pan to form crust.

3 Bake 14 to 16 minutes or until set and edges are light golden brown. Cool completely in pan on cooling rack, about 30 minutes.

4 In small bowl, beat cream cheese, sugar and remaining ½ teaspoon vanilla with electric mixer on medium speed until smooth. Spread mixture over crust. Arrange fruit over filling. Stir or beat jelly with whisk until smooth; spoon or brush over fruit.

5 Refrigerate until chilled, at least 1 hour. Run knife around edge to loosen. Cut into 6 rows by 4 rows. Store covered in refrigerator.

1 Serving: Calories 150; Total Fat 5g (Saturated Fat 2.5g, Trans Fat 0g); Cholesterol 20mg; Sodium 160mg; Total Carbohydrate 23g (Dietary Fiber 0g); Protein 1g **Exchanges:** ½ Starch, 1 Other Carbohydrate, 1 Fat **Carbohydrate Choices:** 1½

Sweet Success Any of your favorite fruits can be used on this colorful pizza. Try raspberries, blackberries, sliced fresh peaches or bananas.

Cooking Gluten Free? Always read labels to make sure each recipe ingredient is gluten free. Products and ingredient sources can change.

Union Jack Fruit Pizza

20 servings | Prep Time: 20 Minutes | Start to Finish: 2 Hours 10 Minutes

CRUST

- 1 pouch (1 lb 1.5 oz) sugar cookie mix
- ½ cup butter, softened
- 1 egg

FILLING

- 1 package (8 oz) cream cheese, softened
- ⅓ cup sugar
- ½ teaspoon vanilla

TOPPING

- 4 cups sliced fresh strawberries
- 3 cups fresh blueberries
- 1 cup fresh raspberries

1. Heat oven to 350°F. Line 15x10x1-inch jelly roll pan with foil, leaving foil overhanging at 2 opposite sides of pan; spray foil with cooking spray.

2. In large bowl, stir crust ingredients until soft dough forms. Press dough in bottom of pan.

3. Bake 15 to 20 minutes or until light golden brown. Cool completely in pan on cooling rack, about 30 minutes. Use foil to lift crust from pan to serving plate.

4. In small bowl, beat cream cheese, sugar and vanilla with electric mixer on medium speed until fluffy. Spread mixture over crust. Arrange fruit over filling to look like Union Jack flag.

5. Refrigerate at least 1 hour until chilled. Cut into 5 rows by 4 rows. Store covered in refrigerator.

1 Serving: Calories 230; Total Fat 11g (Saturated Fat 6g, Trans Fat 1g); Cholesterol 35mg; Sodium 140mg; Total Carbohydrate 29g (Dietary Fiber 1g); Protein 2g **Exchanges:** 1½ Starch, ½ Other Carbohydrate, 2 Fat **Carbohydrate Choices:** 2

The Wow Factor For added shine and sweetness, in small microwavable bowl, mix ½ cup orange, peach or apricot preserves and 1 tablespoon water. Microwave uncovered on High 30 seconds; stir until smooth. Brush over fruit after arranging on filling.

Pumpkin Cheesecake Dessert

16 servings | Prep Time: 20 Minutes | Start to Finish: 3 Hours

BASE

- 1 cup all-purpose flour
- ¾ cup packed brown sugar
- ½ cup butter
- 1 cup quick-cooking oats
- ½ cup finely chopped walnuts

FILLING

- 1 package (8 oz) cream cheese, softened
- ¾ cup granulated sugar
- 1 can (15 oz) pumpkin (not pumpkin pie mix)
- 1½ teaspoons ground cinnamon
- 1 teaspoon ground ginger
- 3 eggs

TOPPING

- 2 cups sour cream
- ⅓ cup granulated sugar
- ½ teaspoon vanilla
- Additional finely chopped walnuts, if desired

1 Heat oven to 350°F. Spray bottom and sides of 13x9-inch pan with cooking spray.

2 In medium bowl, mix flour and brown sugar. Cut in butter, using pastry blender or fork, until mixture looks like coarse crumbs. Stir in oats and ½ cup walnuts. Press mixture in bottom of pan. Bake 15 minutes.

3 Meanwhile, in large bowl, beat filling ingredients with electric mixer on medium speed until well blended. Pour over hot base. Bake 20 to 25 minutes or until set and dry in center.

4 In small bowl, mix sour cream, ⅓ cup granulated sugar and the vanilla. Drop mixture by spoonfuls over pumpkin layer; spread evenly over hot filling. Bake about 5 minutes or until topping is set. Cool on cooling rack 30 minutes. Refrigerate 1 hour 30 minutes.

5 Cut into 4 rows by 4 rows. Sprinkle with additional walnuts. Store covered in refrigerator.

1 Serving: Calories 340; Total Fat 19g (Saturated Fat 11g, Trans Fat 0.5g); Cholesterol 50mg; Sodium 110mg; Total Carbohydrate 37g (Dietary Fiber 2g); Protein 4g
Exchanges: 1 Starch, 1½ Other Carbohydrate, 3½ Fat **Carbohydrate Choices:** 2½

Streusel-Topped Sweet Potato Pie Squares

15 squares | Prep Time: 25 Minutes | Start to Finish: 3 Hours 35 Minutes

CRUST

1   Pillsbury™ refrigerated pie crust, softened as directed on box

FILLING

3   cans (15 oz each) sweet potatoes in syrup, drained, mashed

1   can (14 oz) sweetened condensed milk (not evaporated)

3   eggs, beaten

¾   cup half-and-half

2   teaspoons pumpkin pie spice

½   teaspoon salt

TOPPING

½   cup packed brown sugar

½   cup quick-cooking oats

¼   cup all-purpose flour

½   teaspoon ground cinnamon

¼   cup cold butter

GARNISH

1   cup whipping cream

2   tablespoons powdered sugar

1. Heat oven to 400°F. Unroll pie crust in ungreased 13x9-inch pan. Press crust in bottom and ¼ inch up sides of pan, cutting to fit; press seams firmly to seal. Do not prick crust.

2. Bake 10 minutes. Immediately press bubbles down with back of wooden spoon. Reduce oven temperature to 350°F.

3. In large bowl, beat filling ingredients with whisk until blended. Pour over partially baked crust. Bake 40 minutes.

4. Meanwhile, in medium bowl, mix brown sugar, oats, flour and cinnamon. Cut in butter, using pastry blender or fork, until mixture looks like coarse crumbs. Sprinkle over filling.

5. Bake 15 to 20 minutes longer or until knife inserted in center comes out clean (surface may be puffy in spots). Cool completely in pan on cooling rack. Refrigerate at least 2 hours before serving.

6. In chilled medium bowl, beat whipping cream and powdered sugar with electric mixer on high speed until soft peaks form. Cut into 5 rows by 3 rows; serve with whipped cream. Store covered in refrigerator.

1 Square: Calories 400; Total Fat 17g (Saturated Fat 10g, Trans Fat 0g); Cholesterol 90mg; Sodium 270mg; Total Carbohydrate 55g (Dietary Fiber 3g); Protein 6g **Exchanges:** 3 Other Carbohydrate, ½ Milk, ½ Vegetable, 2½ Fat **Carbohydrate Choices:** 3½

Sweet Success You can substitute fresh cooked dark-orange sweet potatoes for the canned version. Two pounds sweet potatoes will yield about 3 cups mashed.

The Wow Factor You can sprinkle the whipped cream with a little ground cinnamon or nutmeg for a spark of spice.

Chocolate-Peanut Butter Dream Squares

24 squares | Prep Time: 20 Minutes | Start to Finish: 2 Hours 5 Minutes

COOKIE CRUST

- 1 pouch (1 lb 1.5 oz) double chocolate chunk cookie mix
- ¼ cup vegetable oil
- 2 tablespoons cold strong brewed coffee or water
- 1 egg

FILLING

- 1 package (8 oz) cream cheese, softened
- ¼ cup sugar
- 1 container (8 oz) frozen whipped topping, thawed (3½ cups)
- 1 bag (9 oz) miniature chocolate-covered peanut butter cup candies, chopped

TOPPING

- ¼ cup creamy peanut butter
- ¼ cup milk
- 2 tablespoons sugar
- 3 oz bittersweet baking chocolate, melted

  Peanuts for topping

1 Heat oven to 350°F. In large bowl, stir crust ingredients until soft dough forms. Spread dough in bottom of ungreased 13x9-inch pan.

2 Bake 12 to 15 minutes or just until set. Cool completely on cooling rack, about 30 minutes.

3 In large bowl, beat cream cheese and ¼ cup sugar with electric mixer on medium speed until smooth. Fold in whipped topping and candies. Spread over cooled baked crust.

4 In small microwavable bowl, beat peanut butter, milk and 2 tablespoons sugar with whisk until smooth. Microwave uncovered on High 30 to 60 seconds, stirring after 30 seconds, until thin enough to drizzle. Drizzle over filling. Drizzle with melted chocolate. Sprinkle with peanuts.

5 Refrigerate about 1 hour or until set. Cut into 6 rows by 4 rows. Store covered in refrigerator.

1 Square: Calories 320; Total Fat 19g (Saturated Fat 8g, Trans Fat 0g); Cholesterol 20mg; Sodium 170mg; Total Carbohydrate 31g (Dietary Fiber 2g); Protein 5g **Exchanges:** ½ Starch, 1½ Other Carbohydrate, ½ High-Fat Meat, 3 Fat **Carbohydrate Choices:** 2

Peppermint-French Silk Pie Squares

24 squares | Prep Time: 25 Minutes | Start to Finish: 3 Hours 10 Minutes

1 Pillsbury refrigerated pie crust, softened as directed on box

6 oz unsweetened baking chocolate, coarsely chopped

1½ cups butter, softened

2 cups sugar

1 teaspoon peppermint extract

1½ cups fat-free egg product

1 container (8 oz) frozen whipped topping, thawed (3½ cups)

1 Heat oven to 450°F. Unroll crust; place in 13x9-inch pan. Press crust in bottom, cutting to fit; moisten seams with finger dipped in water, and press seams firmly to seal. Press any cutoff dough into dough in center of pan, using same method. DO NOT PRICK CRUST.

2 Bake 11 to 13 minutes or until golden brown. Cool completely on cooling rack, about 30 minutes.

3 Meanwhile, in small microwavable bowl, microwave chocolate uncovered on High 1 to 2 minutes, stirring every 30 seconds, until melted; stir until smooth. Cool 10 minutes.

4 In large bowl, beat butter and sugar with electric mixer on medium speed about 3 minutes or until light and fluffy. Beat in peppermint extract and melted chocolate. Gradually beat in egg product on high speed about 3 minutes or until light and fluffy. Spread filling over cooled baked crust.

5 Refrigerate uncovered about 2 hours or until set. Spread whipped topping over filling. Cut into 6 rows by 4 rows. Store covered in refrigerator.

1 Square: Calories 290; Total Fat 19g (Saturated Fat 12g, Trans Fat 0g); Cholesterol 30mg; Sodium 170mg; Total Carbohydrate 25g (Dietary Fiber 1g); Protein 3g **Exchanges:** 1½ Starch, 3½ Fat **Carbohydrate Choices:** 1½

The Wow Factor For an extra-festive look, top this dessert with crushed peppermint candies and more chopped unsweetened baking chocolate.

Refrigerated and Frozen Desserts

Malted Milk Chocolate Cheesecake

18 servings | Prep Time: 25 Minutes | Start to Finish: 5 Hours 20 Minutes

5   packages (8 oz each) cream cheese, softened

1½   cups sugar

1   cup chocolate-flavor malted milk powder

½   cup unsweetened baking cocoa

1   container (8 oz) sour cream

2   teaspoons vanilla

¼   teaspoon salt

5   eggs

1   cup whipping cream

½   cup chopped chocolate-covered malted milk balls

1 Heat oven to 350°F. Line bottom only of 13x9-inch pan with foil; spray foil with cooking spray. In large bowl, beat cream cheese with electric mixer on medium speed until light and fluffy.

2 In medium bowl, mix sugar, malted milk powder and cocoa. Add to cream cheese; beat on low speed until combined. Beat on medium speed until smooth. Beat in sour cream, vanilla and salt. Add eggs, one at a time, beating just until combined after each addition. Pour batter into pan.

3 Place pan in larger shallow pan in oven.* Add hot water to shallow pan until half full. Bake 50 to 55 minutes or until set.

4 Remove pan from water bath; place on cooling rack. Cool until lukewarm, about 1 hour. Invert cheesecake onto cookie sheet; remove pan and foil. Refrigerate at least 3 hours or overnight.

5 In chilled small bowl, beat whipping cream with electric mixer until stiff peaks form. Cut cheesecake into 6 rows by 3 rows. Garnish with whipped cream and chopped malted milk balls. Store covered in refrigerator.

*The bottom of an oven broiler pan works well for the shallow pan in this recipe.

1 Serving: Calories 420; Total Fat 31g (Saturated Fat 19g, Trans Fat 1g); Cholesterol 150mg; Sodium 260mg; Total Carbohydrate 27g (Dietary Fiber 0g); Protein 8g **Exchanges:** ½ Starch, 1½ Other Carbohydrate, 1 Medium-Fat Meat, 5 Fat **Carbohydrate Choices:** 2

Sweet Success Cheesecake freezes well. Place the leftovers in a freezer container; seal tightly and freeze up to 3 months.

Make It a Wow — Easy Garnish Ideas

The beauty of refrigerated and frozen desserts is that you can make them ahead, taking some of the stress out of entertaining or having dessert on hand for your family for whenever their sweet tooth calls. Here are some cleverly-easy ideas to garnish them, sure to make your guests oooh and ahhh.

Decadent Drizzle

Drizzle servings of dessert with melted chocolate, ice-cream toppings, fruit sauces or jam or jelly that's been softened slightly in the microwave. You can drizzle the plate before placing the dessert on it or drizzle over the dessert on the plate. If you like, add some bite-size pieces of fruit for an extra pop of color.

Crazy for Candy

Top desserts with mini chocolate candy bars, malted milk balls, small candies, mini peanut butter cups, coarsely chopped or crushed hard candies. Mix and match them for a really indulgent look. Place candies on frozen desserts before freezing so they will stick to the top of the dessert. Refrigerate the frozen dessert 15 to 30 minutes before serving to soften the dessert slightly before serving. Place candies on refrigerated desserts just before serving.

Yummy Dippers

Any of these foods make perfect chocolate dippers to garnish desserts. After dipping them, you can sprinkle them with finely chopped nuts, cookie crumbs or sprinkles before placing on cookie sheet to set.

Crisply cooked bacon slices
Crispy horn-shaped corn snacks
Dried fruit (bite-size pieces)
Marshmallows
Pretzels
Small cookies or crackers
Whole strawberries

Chocolate-Dipped Treats

Top your desserts with some sweets that have been dipped in chocolate (see left for delicious foods to dip). You can make these ahead of time, too, and simply top pieces with them when they are served. Melt 1 cup dark or semisweet chocolate chips with 1 teaspoon shortening in small saucepan over low heat, stirring constantly, until melted; remove from heat. Dip dippers about three-fourths of the way into chocolate. Place on cookie sheet lined with waxed paper. Refrigerate about 10 minutes to set; chill until serving.

Sugared Herbs and Fruit

Lightly brush woody herb sprigs, cranberries or grapes with light corn syrup; place on a 15x10x1-inch jelly roll pan lined with parchment or waxed paper. Sprinkle with granulated or decorator sugar crystals. Let stand uncovered up to 1 hour to dry.

Simply Sweet

Sprinkle refrigerated desserts with chocolate chips, chopped nuts, bite-size pieces of fresh fruit (a variety of colors and shapes adds interest), whipped cream and sprinkles. Add just before serving.

Chocolate Overload

Top desserts with chocolate curls, shavings or grated chocolate. Use a room-temperature milk or semisweet chocolate bar. Pull swivel vegetable peeler or thin, sharp knife across bar using long, thin strokes. Lift curls with a toothpick. (To make chocolate shavings, use shorter strokes.) Use cheese grater to make grated chocolate.

Gluten-Free Crispy Strawberry Ice Cream Sandwiches

6 ice cream sandwiches | Prep Time: 15 Minutes | Start to Finish: 2 Hours 15 Minutes

5 cups miniature marshmallows

½ cup unsalted butter, cut into pieces

½ teaspoon salt

5 cups Rice Chex™ cereal, coarsely crushed

3 cups strawberry ice cream, softened

1 Line bottom of 13x9-inch pan and cookie sheet with cooking parchment paper.

2 In 3-quart saucepan, heat 4 cups of the marshmallows, the butter and salt over low heat about 8 minutes, stirring constantly, until melted. Stir in cereal until almost coated; stir in remaining 1 cup marshmallows. Using greased rubber spatula, evenly scrape mixture into pan and spread evenly. Refrigerate about 30 minutes or until easy to handle.

3 Turn pan upside down to remove cereal layer; peel off parchment paper. Cut into 4 rows by 3 rows. Working quickly, spread ½ cup ice cream onto 1 cereal rectangle; top with another rectangle. Repeat with remaining rectangles and ice cream. Place on cookie sheet.

4 Freeze at least 1 hour 30 minutes until firm. Wrap sandwiches individually in plastic wrap; store in freezer.

1 Ice Cream Sandwich: Calories 500; Total Fat 23g (Saturated Fat 14g, Trans Fat 1g); Cholesterol 70mg; Sodium 490mg; Total Carbohydrate 69g (Dietary Fiber 0g); Protein 5g **Exchanges:** 1½ Starch, 3 Other Carbohydrate, 4½ Fat **Carbohydrate Choices:** 4½

Cooking Gluten Free? Always read labels to make sure each recipe ingredient is gluten free. Products and ingredient sources can change.

Layered Raspberry-Chocolate Squares

20 squares | Prep Time: 15 Minutes | Start to Finish: 6 Hours 45 Minutes

CRUST

- 2 cups crushed chocolate wafer cookies (about 32 cookies)
- ⅓ cup butter, melted
- ¼ cup sugar

FILLING

- 1 cup chocolate fudge topping, slightly softened
- 1 quart (4 cups) vanilla ice cream, slightly softened
- 1 pint (2 cups) raspberry sherbet, slightly softened
- 1 bag (12 oz) frozen raspberries
- 1 container (8 oz) frozen whipped topping, thawed

1 In medium bowl, mix crust ingredients; reserve ¼ cup for topping. Press remaining mixture in bottom of ungreased 13x9-inch pan to form crust. Refrigerate 15 minutes.

2 Spread chocolate fudge topping over crust. Spoon vanilla ice cream over chocolate layer. Place spoonfuls of sherbet randomly over ice cream; swirl gently into ice cream. Top with raspberries; press gently into sherbet. Spread whipped topping over raspberry/sherbet layer; sprinkle with reserved crumbs.

3 Cover; freeze 6 hours or overnight. Remove from freezer 10 to 15 minutes before serving. Cut into 5 rows by 4 rows. Store covered in freezer.

1 Square: Calories 260; Total Fat 12g (Saturated Fat 7g, Trans Fat 0.5g); Cholesterol 20mg; Sodium 170mg; Total Carbohydrate 36g (Dietary Fiber 3g); Protein 3g **Exchanges:** 1 Starch, 1½ Other Carbohydrate, 2 Fat **Carbohydrate Choices:** 2½

The Wow Factor Make it look like a fancy restaurant dessert by dusting the dessert plates with finely crushed chocolate wafer crumbs before placing the dessert squares on them. Garnish with a few fresh berries.

Gluten-Free Lime-Vanilla Freeze

15 servings | Prep Time: 15 Minutes | Start to Finish: 5 Hours 15 Minutes

1 box (15 oz) gluten-free yellow cake mix

½ cup finely chopped pecans

¾ cup butter, softened

1 quart (4 cups) lime sherbet, slightly softened

1 quart (4 cups) vanilla ice cream, slightly softened

1 cup frozen (thawed) whipped topping

¼ cup chopped pecans

1 Heat oven to 350°F. Line 13x9-inch pan with foil, leaving foil overhanging at 2 opposite sides of pan.

2 In medium bowl, stir together cake mix and ½ cup pecans. Cut in butter, using pastry blender or fork, until mixture is crumbly. Lightly press mixture in bottom of pan.

3 Bake 15 to 20 minutes or until set and just beginning to brown. Cool completely in pan on cooling rack, about 30 minutes.

4 In large bowl, fold sherbet into ice cream just until partially blended for marbled design. Spoon and spread over crust. Cover; freeze at least 4 hours until firm.

5 Use foil to lift dessert from pan to cutting board 10 minutes before serving; peel back foil. Cut into 5 rows by 3 rows. Garnish with whipped topping and pecans.

1 Serving: Calories 370; Total Fat 19g (Saturated Fat 10g, Trans Fat 0.5g); Cholesterol 40mg; Sodium 270mg; Total Carbohydrate 47g (Dietary Fiber 1g); Protein 3g **Exchanges:** 1½ Starch, 1½ Other Carbohydrate, 3½ Fat **Carbohydrate Choices:** 3

The Wow Factor Substitute your favorite flavor of sherbet, such as raspberry, lemon or orange, for the lime. Garnish with fresh berries.

Cooking Gluten Free? Always read labels to make sure each recipe ingredient is gluten free. Products and ingredient sources can change.

Frozen Tiramisu Squares

15 squares | Prep Time: 20 Minutes | Start to Finish: 5 Hours 35 Minutes

1 cup Original Bisquick™ mix

½ cup sugar

⅓ cup unsweetened baking cocoa

1 tablespoon instant espresso coffee powder or granules

⅓ cup butter, melted

2 packages (8 oz each) cream cheese, softened

1 can (14 oz) sweetened condensed milk (not evaporated)

¼ cup frozen (thawed) orange juice concentrate

1 teaspoon instant espresso coffee powder or granules

1 tablespoon hot water

¼ cup chocolate-flavor syrup

1½ cups whipping cream

Additional unsweetened baking cocoa, if desired

1 Heat oven to 350°F. Grease bottom and sides of 13x9-inch pan with shortening or cooking spray.

2 In medium bowl, stir together Bisquick mix, sugar, ⅓ cup cocoa, 1 tablespoon espresso powder and the butter until crumbly. Crumble mixture lightly into pan. Bake 6 minutes. Cool.

3 In medium bowl, beat cream cheese with electric mixer on medium speed until smooth. Gradually beat in milk. Spoon about 2 cups of the cream cheese mixture into separate bowl; stir in orange juice concentrate. Dissolve 1 teaspoon espresso powder in hot water; stir coffee mixture and chocolate syrup into cream cheese mixture in other bowl.

4 In chilled medium bowl, beat whipping cream on high speed until stiff peaks form. Fold half of the whipped cream into each cream cheese mixture. Refrigerate chocolate mixture. Spoon orange mixture over crust; freeze about 1 hour or until firm. Spread chocolate mixture evenly over orange mixture.

5 Freeze about 4 hours or until firm. Remove from freezer 10 minutes before serving. Cut into 5 rows by 3 rows. Sprinkle with additional cocoa. Store covered in freezer.

1 Square: Calories 400; Total Fat 26g (Saturated Fat 16g, Trans Fat 1g); Cholesterol 85mg; Sodium 270mg; Total Carbohydrate 35g (Dietary Fiber 1g); Protein 5g **Exchanges:** 1½ Starch, 1 Other Carbohydrate, 5 Fat **Carbohydrate Choices:** 2

Betty Crocker Sheet Pan Desserts

Brownie Ice Cream Sandwiches

12 ice cream sandwiches | Prep Time: 15 Minutes | Start to Finish: 2 Hours 45 Minutes

1 box (1 lb 6.25 oz) supreme brownie mix with pouch of chocolate-flavor syrup

Water, vegetable oil and eggs called for on brownie mix box

1 quart (4 cups) vanilla ice cream, slightly softened

Assorted sprinkles, chocolate chips and candies, if desired

1 Heat oven to 350°F. Line 13x9-inch pan with foil, leaving foil overhanging at 2 opposite sides of pan; spray foil with cooking spray.

2 In large bowl, stir together brownie mix, water, oil and eggs. Pour batter into pan. Bake 28 to 30 minutes or until toothpick inserted in center comes out almost clean. Cool completely in pan on cooling rack, about 1 hour.

3 Place pan of brownies in freezer 30 minutes. Use foil to lift brownies from pan; peel off foil. Cut into 6 rows by 4 rows.

4 For each sandwich, spoon about ¼ cup ice cream on bottom of 1 brownie rectangle. Top with second brownie rectangle, bottom side down; gently press together. Roll sides in sprinkles. Place in shallow pan.

5 Freeze until firm, about 30 minutes. Wrap sandwiches individually in plastic wrap; store in freezer.

1 Ice Cream Sandwich: Calories 390; Total Fat 16g (Saturated Fat 6g, Trans Fat 0g); Cholesterol 50mg; Sodium 240mg; Total Carbohydrate 55g (Dietary Fiber 1g); Protein 4g
Exchanges: 1½ Starch, 2 Other Carbohydrate, 3 Fat **Carbohydrate Choices:** 3½

Turtle Brownie Ice Cream Dessert

20 servings | Prep Time: 15 Minutes | Start to Finish: 4 Hours 20 Minutes

BROWNIES

1   box (1 lb 2.3 oz) fudge brownie mix

     Water, vegetable oil and eggs called for on brownie mix box

½   cup chopped pecans

FILLING

2   quarts (8 cups) dulce de leche ice cream, slightly softened

½   cup hot fudge topping, heated until warm

½   cup chopped pecans

1   cup frozen (thawed) whipped topping, if desired

1. Heat oven to 350°F. Spray bottom only of 15x10x1-inch jelly roll pan with cooking spray.

2. In large bowl, stir brownie mix, water, oil and eggs until well blended. Stir in ½ cup pecans. Spread batter in pan.

3. Bake 15 to 17 minutes or until center is set. Do not overbake. Cool completely in pan on cooling rack, about 45 minutes.

4. Spoon ice cream evenly over brownies; smooth with back of spoon or rubber spatula. Freeze uncovered until firm, about 3 hours.

5. Drizzle hot fudge topping over dessert with fork, using quick strokes. Sprinkle with ½ cup pecans. Let stand at room temperature about 5 minutes before cutting. Cut into 5 rows by 4 rows. Serve with whipped topping. Store covered in freezer.

1 Serving: Calories 350; Total Fat 19g (Saturated Fat 6g, Trans Fat 0g); Cholesterol 45mg; Sodium 160mg; Total Carbohydrate 41g (Dietary Fiber 1g); Protein 3g **Exchanges:** 1 Starch, 1½ Other Carbohydrate, 3½ Fat **Carbohydrate Choices:** 3

Sweet Success Vanilla ice cream can be used in place of the dulce de leche ice cream. Drizzle the dessert with ½ cup caramel topping along with the hot fudge.

Fudge Ice Cream Cake

15 servings | Prep Time: 15 Minutes | Start to Finish: 6 Hours 5 Minutes

1 box (15.25 oz) chocolate fudge cake mix with pudding in the mix

½ cup butter, softened

3 eggs

1 can or jar (16 oz) hot fudge topping, warmed

2 cups chopped creme-filled chocolate sandwich cookies (20 cookies)

1 brick (½ gallon) vanilla ice cream, slightly softened

1 Heat oven to 350°F (325°F for dark or nonstick pan). Line 13x9-inch pan with foil, leaving foil overhanging at 2 opposite sides of pan; spray bottom of foil only with cooking spray.

2 In large bowl, stir cake mix, butter and eggs with spoon until blended (batter will be very thick). Using greased fingers, spread or pat batter in pan.

3 Bake 18 to 21 minutes or until surface appears dry and is no longer shiny. Run knife around side of cake to loosen. Cool completely in pan on cooling rack, about 1 hour.

4 Spread fudge topping over cake; sprinkle with 1 cup of the chopped cookies. Freeze until firm, about 30 minutes. Spread ice cream over cookies.

5 Cover; freeze at least 4 hours until firm. Remove from freezer 15 minutes before serving. Sprinkle with remaining 1 cup chopped cookies. For easier cutting, remove from pan, using foil to lift. Cut into 5 rows by 3 rows. Store covered in freezer.

1 Serving: Calories 500; Total Fat 22g (Saturated Fat 12g, Trans Fat 0.5g); Cholesterol 90mg; Sodium 550mg; Total Carbohydrate 70g (Dietary Fiber 2g); Protein 7g **Exchanges:** 2½ Starch, 2 Other Carbohydrate, 4 Fat **Carbohydrate Choices:** 4½

The Wow Factor Go ahead and use any flavor of ice cream in place of vanilla. Chocolate chip, cookies and cream or cherry are all scrumptious choices.

Sweet Success Don't let the ice cream get overly soft or let it melt. To make it smoother, place in a large bowl and stir with a sturdy wooden spoon before spreading over the cookie layer.

Mud Slide Ice Cream Cake

15 servings | Prep Time: 15 Minutes | Start to Finish: 5 Hours 35 Minutes

1 box (15.25 oz) chocolate fudge cake mix with pudding in the mix

½ cup butter, softened

1 egg

2 tablespoons milk

2 tablespoons coffee-flavored liqueur or cold strong brewed coffee

1 quart (4 cups) vanilla ice cream, slightly softened

1 container (12 oz) chocolate whipped ready-to-spread frosting

2 tablespoons coffee-flavored liqueur, if desired

1 Heat oven to 350°F (325°F for dark or nonstick pan). Grease bottom only of 13x9-inch pan with shortening or cooking spray.

2 In large bowl, beat cake mix, butter, egg and milk with spoon or electric mixer on low speed until well blended. Spread batter in pan.

3 Bake 16 to 18 minutes or until center is set (top may appear dry and cracked). Cool completely in pan on cooling rack, about 1 hour.

4 Brush 2 tablespoons liqueur over cake. Spread ice cream over cake. Freeze about 3 hours or until firm.

5 In medium bowl, mix frosting and 2 tablespoons liqueur; spread over ice cream. Freeze at least 1 hour. Cut into 5 rows by 3 rows. Store covered in freezer.

1 Serving: Calories 340; Total Fat 16g (Saturated Fat 8g, Trans Fat 1.5g); Cholesterol 45mg; Sodium 390mg; Total Carbohydrate 46g (Dietary Fiber 1g); Protein 3g **Exchanges:** 1 Starch, 2 Other Carbohydrate, 3 Fat **Carbohydrate Choices:** 3

White Chocolate–Cherry Ice Cream Cake

16 servings | Prep Time: 25 Minutes | Start to Finish: 5 Hours

1 box (16.25 oz) white cake mix with pudding in the mix

1 box (4-serving size) white chocolate instant pudding and pie filling mix

1 cup water

⅓ cup vegetable oil

4 egg whites

6 cups cherry–chocolate chip ice cream, slightly softened

1 cup whipping cream

1 package (6 oz) white chocolate baking bars, chopped

¼ cup hot fudge topping

1 Heat oven to 350°F (325°F for dark or nonstick pan). Spray bottom only of 13x9-inch pan with baking spray with flour.

2 In large bowl, beat cake mix, dry pudding mix, water, oil and egg whites with electric mixer on low speed 30 seconds, then on medium speed 2 minutes (batter will be very thick). Spread batter in pan.

3 Bake 29 to 35 minutes or until toothpick inserted in center comes out clean. Cool completely in pan on cooling rack, about 1 hour.

4 With serrated knife, cut cake into 1- to 1½-inch squares. In very large bowl, stir ice cream until very soft. Add cake squares; stir until cake is coated (cake pieces will break up). Spoon mixture back into pan. Smooth top. Freeze about 3 hours or until firm.

5 Meanwhile, in 1-quart saucepan, heat whipping cream until hot but not boiling. Stir in chopped white chocolate until melted and smooth. Pour mixture into small bowl. Refrigerate 1 hour 30 minutes to 2 hours or until cold. Beat with electric mixer on high speed until soft peaks form (do not overbeat or mixture will look curdled). Spread over ice-cream cake.

6 In small microwavable bowl, microwave fudge topping uncovered on High about 15 seconds or until melted; stir until smooth. Spoon into small resealable freezer plastic bag; seal bag. Cut small tip off bottom corner of bag; squeeze bag to drizzle topping over cake. Cut into 4 rows by 4 rows. Serve immediately, or cover and freeze.

1 Serving: Calories 400; Total Fat 20g (Saturated Fat 10g, Trans Fat 0g); Cholesterol 40mg; Sodium 370mg; Total Carbohydrate 50g (Dietary Fiber 0g); Protein 5g **Exchanges:** 1½ Starch, 2 Other Carbohydrate, 3½ Fat **Carbohydrate Choices:** 3

Dulce de Leche–Mocha Ice Cream Dessert

16 servings | Prep Time: 45 Minutes | Start to Finish: 6 Hours 45 Minutes

PRALINE CRUMBS

10	graham cracker rectangles
1	cup butter
1	cup packed brown sugar
1	cup chopped pecans

FILLING AND TOPPING

1	quart (4 cups) dulce de leche ice cream, slightly softened
1	can or jar (16 oz) hot fudge topping
1	quart (4 cups) coffee ice cream, slightly softened
1½	cups whipping cream
⅓	cup coffee-flavored liqueur

1 Heat oven to 350°F. Arrange graham crackers in single layer in ungreased 15x10x1-inch jelly roll pan.

2 In 2-quart saucepan, melt butter over medium-high heat. Stir in brown sugar. Heat to boiling; boil 2 minutes. Remove from heat. Stir in pecans. Pour and spread over crackers. Bake 10 minutes. Cool completely in pan on cooling rack, about 30 minutes.

3 Crush crackers into coarse crumbs. Sprinkle half of the crumbs in ungreased 13x9-inch pan. Cut and remove carton from dulce de leche ice cream. Cut ice cream into ½-inch-thick slices. Arrange slices over crumbs, overlapping slightly if necessary. Spread ice cream with spatula until smooth, pressing down firmly. Freeze 1 hour until firm.

4 Pour fudge topping into resealable 1-quart food-storage plastic bag; seal bag. Cut small tip off bottom corner of bag; squeeze bag to pipe topping over ice cream. Sprinkle remaining praline crumbs over fudge layer. Freeze 30 minutes or until fudge is firm.

5 Cut and remove carton from coffee ice cream. Cut ice cream into ½-inch-thick slices. Arrange slices over crumbs, overlapping slightly if necessary. Spread ice cream with spatula until smooth, pressing down firmly. Freeze while preparing topping.

6 In large bowl, beat whipping cream with electric mixer on high speed until stiff peaks form. Fold in liqueur. Spread over dessert.

7 Freeze 4 hours until firm. Remove from freezer 20 minutes before serving. Cut into 4 rows by 4 rows. Store covered in freezer up to 1 week.

1 Serving: Calories 590; Total Fat 35g (Saturated Fat 19g, Trans Fat 1g); Cholesterol 85mg; Sodium 290mg; Total Carbohydrate 61g (Dietary Fiber 2g); Protein 5g **Exchanges:** 0 **Carbohydrate Choices:** 4

CHAPTER TWO

Cakes

White Chocolate Sheet Cake

24 servings | Prep Time: 30 Minutes | Start to Finish: 2 Hours 25 Minutes

CAKE

- 3 oz white chocolate baking bars, chopped
- 2 tablespoons whipping cream
- 1 box (16.25 oz) white cake mix with pudding in the mix
- 1 container (8 oz) sour cream
- ½ cup vegetable oil
- 3 eggs

FROSTING

- 3 oz white chocolate baking bars, chopped
- 3 tablespoons whipping cream
- ½ cup butter, softened
- 3 cups powdered sugar

GARNISH

- ½ cup chopped pecans, toasted* if desired

1 Heat oven to 350°F (325°F for dark or nonstick pan). Spray bottom and sides of 15x10x1-inch jelly roll pan with baking spray with flour.

2 In small microwavable bowl, microwave 3 oz white chocolate and 2 tablespoons whipping cream uncovered on High 1 minute, stirring every 30 seconds, until smooth. Cool 10 to 15 minutes.

3 In large bowl, beat cake mix, sour cream, oil, eggs and white chocolate mixture with electric mixer on low speed 30 seconds, then on medium speed 2 minutes, scraping bowl occasionally. Pour batter into pan.

4 Bake 21 to 25 minutes or until toothpick inserted in center comes out clean. Cool completely in pan on cooling rack, about 1 hour.

5 In small microwavable bowl, microwave 3 oz white chocolate and 3 tablespoons whipping cream uncovered on High 1 minute, stirring every 30 seconds, until smooth. Cool 10 to 15 minutes.

6 In medium bowl, beat butter and 2 cups of the powdered sugar with electric mixer on medium speed until blended. Add white chocolate mixture; blend well. Add remaining 1 cup powdered sugar; beat until smooth. Frost cake; sprinkle with pecans. Store loosely covered.

*To toast pecans, spread in ungreased shallow pan. Bake uncovered at 350°F 6 to 10 minutes, stirring occasionally, until light brown.

1 Serving: Calories 280; Total Fat 15g (Saturated Fat 7g, Trans Fat 0g); Cholesterol 45mg; Sodium 180mg; Total Carbohydrate 35g (Dietary Fiber 0g); Protein 2g **Exchanges:** ½ Starch, 2 Other Carbohydrate, 3 Fat **Carbohydrate Choices:** 2

The Wow Factor Toasting pecans and other nuts intensifies their flavor.

White Chocolate–Coconut Cake

15 servings | Prep Time: 20 Minutes | Start to Finish: 2 Hours

CAKE

1 can (14 oz) coconut milk (not cream of coconut)

1 box (16.25 oz) white cake mix with pudding in the mix

¼ cup water

3 egg whites

¾ cup flaked or shredded coconut

FROSTING

1 cup white vanilla baking chips

1¾ cups powdered sugar

⅓ cup butter, softened

½ teaspoon vanilla

1 Heat oven to 350°F (325°F for dark or nonstick pan). Spray bottom only of 13x9-inch pan with baking spray with flour. Reserve ⅓ cup coconut milk for frosting.

2 In large bowl, beat cake mix, remaining coconut milk (1⅓ cups), the water and egg whites with electric mixer on low speed 30 seconds, then on medium speed 2 minutes, scraping bowl occasionally. Stir in ½ cup of the coconut until well combined. Pour batter into pan.

3 Bake as directed on box for 13x9-inch pan. Cool completely in pan on cooling rack, about 1 hour.

4 Meanwhile, in 2-quart microwavable bowl, microwave baking chips uncovered on High about 30 to 45 seconds, stirring once, until melted and chips can be stirred smooth. Stir in powdered sugar, butter, reserved ⅓ cup coconut milk and the vanilla. Cover; refrigerate 30 to 60 minutes. (If frosting becomes too firm to spread, microwave uncovered on High 10 to 15 seconds to soften; stir until smooth.)

5 Frost cake; immediately sprinkle with remaining ¼ cup coconut. Store loosely covered.

1 Serving: Calories 330; Total Fat 13g (Saturated Fat 10g, Trans Fat 0g); Cholesterol 10mg; Sodium 310mg; Total Carbohydrate 51g (Dietary Fiber 0g); Protein 3g **Exchanges:** 1 Starch, 2½ Other Carbohydrate, 2½ Fat **Carbohydrate Choices:** 3½

Jelly Roll Cake

10 servings | Prep Time: 30 Minutes | Start to Finish: 1 Hour 15 Minutes

3   eggs
1   cup granulated sugar
⅓   cup water
1   teaspoon vanilla
¾   cup all-purpose flour
1   teaspoon baking powder
¼   teaspoon salt
    Powdered sugar
    About ⅔ cup jelly or jam

1 Heat oven to 375°F. Line 15x10x1-inch jelly roll pan with waxed paper, cooking parchment paper or foil; generously grease paper or foil with shortening.

2 In medium bowl, beat eggs with electric mixer on high speed about 5 minutes or until very thick and lemon colored. Gradually beat in granulated sugar. On low speed, beat in water and vanilla. Gradually add flour, baking powder and salt, beating just until smooth. Pour batter into pan, spreading to corners.

3 Bake 12 to 15 minutes or until toothpick inserted in center comes out clean. Immediately run knife around sides of pan to loosen cake; turn upside down onto towel generously sprinkled with powdered sugar. Carefully remove paper or foil. Trim off stiff edges of cake if necessary. While cake is hot, carefully roll cake and towel from narrow end. Cool on cooling rack at least 30 minutes.

4 Unroll cake and remove towel. Beat jelly slightly with fork to soften; spread over cake. Roll up cake. Sprinkle with powdered sugar.

1 Serving: Calories 200; Total Fat 1.5g (Saturated Fat 0.5g, Trans Fat 0g); Cholesterol 65mg; Sodium 135mg; Total Carbohydrate 42g (Dietary Fiber 0g); Protein 3g **Exchanges:** 1 Starch, 2 Other Carbohydrate **Carbohydrate Choices:** 3

Chocolate Cake Roll Increase eggs to 4. Beat in ¼ cup unsweetened baking cocoa with the flour. If desired, fill cake with ice cream instead of jelly. Spread 1 to 1½ pints (2 to 3 cups) slightly softened ice cream over cooled cake. Roll as directed; wrap in plastic wrap. Freeze about 4 hours or until firm.

Lemon Curd Cake Roll Add 2 teaspoons grated lemon peel to batter with the flour. Omit jelly; spread cake with ⅔ cup lemon curd. Roll as directed. Store covered in refrigerator.

Whipped Cream Cake Roll
Substitute ½ teaspoon almondextract for the vanilla. Omit jelly. In chilled small bowl, beat ½ cup whipping cream, 2 teaspoons powdered sugar and ¼ teaspoon almond extract with electric mixer on low speed until mixture begins to thicken. Gradually increase speed to high and beat just until stiff peaks form. Spread over cake. Roll as directed. Store covered in refrigerator.

Caramel Apple Cake

12 servings | Prep Time: 15 Minutes | Start to Finish: 2 Hours 5 Minutes

1   box (16.25 oz) white cake mix with pudding in the mix

    Water, vegetable oil and egg whites called for on cake mix box

1   cup caramel topping

2   small red apples

2   tablespoons orange juice

¼   cup chopped nuts, if desired

1   container (16 oz) chocolate creamy ready-to-spread frosting

1 Heat oven to 350°F (325°F for dark or nonstick pan). Make and bake cake as directed on box for 13x9-inch pan, using water, oil and egg whites. Cool 15 minutes.

2 With end of wooden spoon handle, poke holes halfway into cake every 2 inches; evenly pour ¾ cup of the caramel topping over holes. Cool completely in pan on cooling rack, about 1 hour.

3 Cut each apple into 6 wedges. Dip cut edges into orange juice to prevent browning; slightly pat dry. Dip uncut edges into remaining ¼ cup caramel topping; roll in nuts. Cover; refrigerate until serving time.

4 Frost cake with chocolate frosting. Just before serving, place an apple wedge on each piece of cake. Store loosely covered.

1 Serving: Calories 430; Total Fat 13g (Saturated Fat 3.5g, Trans Fat 2g); Cholesterol 0mg; Sodium 480mg; Total Carbohydrate 75g (Dietary Fiber 1g); Protein 3g **Exchanges:** 1 Starch, 4 Other Carbohydrate, 2½ Fat **Carbohydrate Choices:** 5

Sweet Success Use small crab apples with stems, if they're available, for a super-cute garnish instead of the apple wedges. There's no need for the orange juice, and everyone gets an apple!

Tres Leches Cake

15 servings | Prep Time: 30 Minutes | Start to Finish: 4 Hours 5 Minutes

CAKE

2¼	cups all-purpose flour
1½	cups sugar
3½	teaspoons baking powder
½	teaspoon salt
½	cup butter, softened
1¼	cups milk
1	teaspoon vanilla
3	eggs

TOPPING

2	cups whipping cream
1	cup whole milk
1	can (14 oz) sweetened condensed milk (not evaporated)
⅓	cup rum or 1 tablespoon rum extract plus enough water to measure ⅓ cup
2	tablespoons rum or 1 teaspoon rum extract
½	teaspoon vanilla
½	cup chopped pecans, toasted*

1 Heat oven to 350°F. Grease bottom only of 13x9-inch pan with shortening.

2 In large bowl, beat cake ingredients with electric mixer on low speed 30 seconds, scraping bowl constantly. Beat on high speed 3 minutes, scraping bowl occasionally. Pour batter into pan.

3 Bake 25 to 30 minutes or until toothpick inserted in center comes out clean or cake springs back when touched lightly in center. Cool 5 minutes.

4 With long-tined fork, pierce top of hot cake every ½ inch, wiping fork occasionally to reduce sticking. In large bowl, stir 1 cup of the whipping cream, the whole milk, condensed milk and ⅓ cup rum until well mixed. Carefully pour milk mixture evenly over top of cake. Cover; refrigerate about 3 hours or until chilled and most of milk mixture has been absorbed into cake (when cutting cake to serve, you may notice some of the milk mixture on bottom of pan).

5 In chilled large deep bowl, beat remaining 1 cup whipping cream, 2 tablespoons rum and ½ teaspoon vanilla with electric mixer on low speed until mixture begins to thicken. Gradually increase speed to high and beat just until soft peaks form. Frost cake with whipped cream mixture. Sprinkle with pecans. Store covered in refrigerator.

*To toast pecans, spread in ungreased shallow pan. Bake uncovered at 350°F 6 to 10 minutes, stirring occasionally, until light brown.

1 Serving: Calories 480; Total Fat 25g (Saturated Fat 14g, Trans Fat 1g); Cholesterol 110mg; Sodium 320mg; Total Carbohydrate 52g (Dietary Fiber 1g); Protein 7g
Carbohydrate Choices: 3½

Tropical Tres Leches Cake
Make cake as directed—except omit pecans. Sprinkle frosted cake with 1 cup toasted coconut and ½ cup chopped toasted macadamia nuts.

Easy Tiramisu

15 servings | Prep Time: 25 Minutes | Start to Finish: 2 Hours 20 Minutes

CAKE

1   box (16.25 oz) white cake mix with pudding in the mix

1   cup water

⅓   cup vegetable oil

¼   cup brandy or 1½ teaspoons brandy extract plus ¼ cup water

3   egg whites

ESPRESSO SYRUP

¼   cup instant espresso coffee powder or granules

½   cup boiling water

2   tablespoons corn syrup

TOPPING

1   package (8 oz) cream cheese, softened

½   cup powdered sugar

2   cups whipping cream

1   tablespoon unsweetened baking cocoa, if desired

1 Heat oven to 350°F (325°F for dark or nonstick pan). Grease bottom only of 13x9-inch pan with shortening or cooking spray.

2 In large bowl, beat cake ingredients with electric mixer on low speed 30 seconds, then on medium speed 2 minutes, scraping bowl occasionally. Pour batter into pan.

3 Bake 34 to 39 minutes or until toothpick inserted in center comes out clean or cake springs back when touched lightly in center. Cool 15 minutes.

4 With long-tined fork, pierce top of warm cake every ½ inch. In small bowl, mix espresso powder and boiling water. Stir in corn syrup. Brush espresso syrup over top of cake. Cool completely in pan on cooling rack, about 1 hour.

5 In medium bowl, beat cream cheese and powdered sugar with electric mixer on low speed until mixed. Beat on high speed until smooth. Gradually add whipping cream, beating on high speed about 2 minutes or until stiff peaks form. Spread mixture over top of cake; sprinkle with cocoa. Store covered in refrigerator.

1 Serving: Calories 360; Total Fat 23g (Saturated Fat 12g, Trans Fat 0.5g); Cholesterol 60mg; Sodium 290mg; Total Carbohydrate 33g (Dietary Fiber 0g); Protein 3g **Exchanges:** 1 Starch, 1 Other Carbohydrate, 4½ Fat **Carbohydrate Choices:** 2

Sweet Success Place the cocoa in a small, fine-mesh strainer. Hold it over the Tiramisu and tap the edge of the strainer with a spoon to evenly sprinkle the cocoa.

Marble Cake

12 servings | Prep Time: 50 Minutes | Start to Finish: 2 Hours 35 Minutes

CAKE

2¼	cups all-purpose flour or 2½ cups cake flour
1⅔	cups sugar
3½	teaspoons baking powder
1	teaspoon salt
⅔	cup shortening
1¼	cups milk
1	teaspoon vanilla or almond extract
5	egg whites
3	tablespoons unsweetened baking cocoa
⅛	teaspoon baking soda

FROSTING

2	egg whites
½	cup sugar
¼	cup light corn syrup
2	tablespoons water
1	teaspoon vanilla

1 Heat oven to 350°F. Grease bottom and sides of 13x9-inch pan with shortening; lightly flour.

2 In large bowl, beat flour, 1⅔ cups sugar, the baking powder, salt, shortening, milk and 1 teaspoon vanilla with electric mixer on low speed 30 seconds, scraping bowl constantly. Beat on high speed 2 minutes, scraping bowl occasionally. Add 5 egg whites; beat on high speed 2 minutes, scraping bowl occasionally.

3 Remove 1¾ cups of the batter to small bowl. Pour remaining batter into pan. Add cocoa and baking soda to batter in bowl; mix well. Drop chocolate batter by tablespoonfuls randomly onto white batter; cut through batters with knife for marbled design.

4 Bake 40 to 45 minutes or until toothpick inserted in center comes out clean or cake springs back when touched lightly in center. Cool completely in pan on cooling rack, about 1 hour.

5 Meanwhile, let 2 egg whites stand at room temperature for 30 minutes. In medium bowl, beat egg whites with electric mixer on high speed just until stiff peaks form.

6 In 1-quart saucepan, stir ½ cup sugar, the corn syrup and water until well mixed. Cover; heat to rolling boil over medium heat. Uncover; boil 4 to 8 minutes, without stirring, to 242°F on candy thermometer or until small amount of mixture dropped into cup of very cold water forms a firm ball that holds its shape until pressed. (For an accurate temperature reading, tilt the saucepan slightly so mixture is deep enough for thermometer.)

7 Pour hot syrup very slowly in thin stream into egg whites, beating constantly on medium speed. Add 1 teaspoon vanilla. Beat on high speed about 10 minutes or until stiff peaks form. Frost cake. Store loosely covered in refrigerator.

1 Serving: Calories 380; Total Fat 12g (Saturated Fat 3.5g, Trans Fat 0g); Cholesterol 0mg; Sodium 400mg; Total Carbohydrate 62g (Dietary Fiber 1g); Protein 5g **Exchanges:** 1 Starch, 3 Other Carbohydrate, 2½ Fat **Carbohydrate Choices:** 4

Triple-Chocolate Sheet Cake

24 servings | Prep Time: 15 Minutes | Start to Finish: 1 Hour 25 Minutes

1 box (15.25 oz) devil's food or butter recipe chocolate cake mix with pudding in the mix

½ cup sour cream

1 cup water

2 tablespoons unsweetened baking cocoa

2 tablespoons vegetable oil or softened butter

3 eggs

1 container (16 oz) chocolate creamy ready-to-spread frosting

¾ cup chopped pecans

1 Heat oven to 350°F (325°F for dark or nonstick pan). Spray bottom and sides of 15x10x1-inch jelly roll pan with baking spray with flour.

2 In large bowl, beat cake mix, sour cream, water, cocoa, oil and eggs with electric mixer on low speed 30 seconds, then on medium speed 2 minutes, scraping bowl occasionally. Pour batter into pan.

3 Bake 18 to 22 minutes or until toothpick inserted in center comes out clean. Cool completely in pan on cooling rack, about 45 minutes.

4 Spoon frosting into small microwavable bowl. Microwave uncovered on High 20 to 30 seconds, stirring once, until pourable. Pour and spread frosting over cake. Sprinkle with pecans.

1 Serving: Calories 190; Total Fat 8g (Saturated Fat 3g, Trans Fat 1g); Cholesterol 30mg; Sodium 220mg; Total Carbohydrate 27g (Dietary Fiber 1g); Protein 2g **Exchanges:** ½ Starch, 1½ Other Carbohydrate, 1½ Fat **Carbohydrate Choices:** 2

Nut-Topped Chocolate Cake

12 servings | Prep Time: 20 Minutes | Start to Finish: 2 Hours 5 Minutes

CAKE

- 1 box (15.25 oz) devil's food cake mix with pudding in the mix
- 2 tablespoons unsweetened baking cocoa
- 1¼ cups buttermilk
- ½ cup vegetable oil
- 3 eggs

FROSTING AND TOPPING

- ½ cup butter
- 1 cup packed brown sugar
- ¼ cup milk
- 2 cups powdered sugar
- ½ cup chocolate-covered cashews
- ½ cup coarsely chopped cashews
- ½ cup coarsely chopped candied pecans

1 Heat oven to 350°F (325°F for dark or nonstick pan). Spray bottom only of 13x9-inch pan with baking spray with flour.

2 In large bowl, beat cake ingredients with electric mixer on low speed 30 seconds, then on medium speed 2 minutes, scraping bowl occasionally. Pour batter into pan.

3 Bake 35 to 43 minutes or until toothpick inserted in center comes out clean. Cool completely in pan on cooling rack, about 1 hour.

4 Meanwhile, in 2-quart saucepan, melt butter over medium heat. Stir in brown sugar. Heat to boiling, stirring constantly. Reduce heat to low; boil 2 minutes, stirring constantly. Stir in milk; return to boiling. Remove from heat. Cool to lukewarm, about 30 minutes.

5 Gradually stir powdered sugar into brown sugar mixture. Place saucepan of frosting in bowl of cold water; beat with spoon until smooth and spreadable. If frosting becomes too stiff, stir in additional milk, 1 teaspoon at a time, or heat over low heat, stirring constantly. Frost cake. Sprinkle with cashews and pecans. Store loosely covered.

1 Serving: Calories 590; Total Fat 29g (Saturated Fat 10g, Trans Fat 0g); Cholesterol 75mg; Sodium 420mg; Total Carbohydrate 74g (Dietary Fiber 2g); Protein 6g
Exchanges: 1½ Starch, 3½ Other Carbohydrate, 5½ Fat **Carbohydrate Choices:** 5

German Chocolate Sheet Cake

24 servings | Prep Time: 15 Minutes | Start to Finish: 1 Hour 30 Minutes

CAKE

1   box (15.25 oz) German chocolate cake mix with pudding in the mix

     Water, vegetable oil and eggs called for on cake mix box

1   can (14 oz) sweetened condensed milk (not evaporated)

½   cup flaked coconut

½   cup chopped pecans

FROSTING

½   cup butter, softened

4   cups powdered sugar

⅓   cup unsweetened baking cocoa

1   teaspoon vanilla

⅓   cup milk

1   Heat oven to 350°F (325°F for dark or nonstick pan). Spray 15x10x1-inch jelly roll pan with cooking spray.

2   Make cake mix as directed on box, using water, oil and eggs. Pour batter into pan. Bake 15 minutes.

3   Set oven control to broil. In medium bowl, mix condensed milk, coconut and pecans; spread over warm cake. Broil on lowest oven rack about 2 minutes or until golden. Cool completely in pan on cooling rack, about 1 hour.

4   In large bowl, beat butter, powdered sugar, cocoa and vanilla with electric mixer on medium speed until blended. Gradually add milk, beating until frosting is smooth and spreadable. Frost cake. Store covered in refrigerator.

1 Serving: Calories 230; Total Fat 5g (Saturated Fat 1.5g, Trans Fat 0g); Cholesterol 0mg; Sodium 190mg; Total Carbohydrate 45g (Dietary Fiber 1g); Protein 3g **Exchanges:** ½ Starch, 2½ Other Carbohydrate, ½ Fat **Carbohydrate Choices:** 3

Dump Cakes Reinvented

What is a dump cake? Traditionally it's a few ingredients "dumped" in a pan—a can of fruit pie filling, a box of dry cake mix and a little liquid. Easy? Absolutely, but the resulting baked cakes might be described as sickeningly sweet with no fresh flavor and pockets of dry cake mix sitting on top—not the most delicious dessert to eat.

Not anymore. We've come up with a more delicious way to make them. Our reinvented dump cakes start with fresh or frozen fruit, making them the perfect choice for when you have seasonal fruit on hand. The fruit is then topped with just the right amount of Master Scratch Dump Cake Mix (see page 76). (You can make enough mix for one dump cake or enough to have on hand for several dump cakes, whenever you want to whip one up.) They are still a cinch to put together, but now they have irresistible flavor and are the perfect ratio of fruit to topping—think (or don't think) easy yumminess.

Irresistible Dump Cake Toppers

The simplicity of dump cakes calls for equally simple garnishes—try one of these easy toppings:

SCOOP of ice cream

DOLLOP of whipped cream

DRIZZLE of chocolate or caramel ice cream topping

SPRINKLE with chopped nuts

Secrets to a Great Dump Cake

- **SPRAY THE PAN** The fruit and sugar can cause stuck spots on your pan, making it harder to serve nice portions and to clean the pan.

- **START WITH FRESH OR FROZEN FRUIT** If using frozen, in some cases it's better to leave it frozen so the fruit shape will stay intact during baking (like raspberries). In other cases, the fruit may need to be thawed before using so that it will bake in the time it takes to get the topping done. See individual recipes for which form to use.

- **CONTROL THE CAKE MIX** Too much cake mix leaves dry spots on the baked dessert and an overpowering flavor that doesn't allow the fruit flavor to shine. Use one single recipe of our Master Scratch Dump Cake mix (2 cups) or ½ packaged yellow cake mix (about 1½ cups).

- **ADD TEXTURE** Add additional ingredients that add texture to the dump cake. Oats, nuts, crystallized ginger or coarse sugar can be sprinkled on top. It's amazing what just a touch of texture can contribute to the eating experience.

Master Scratch Dump Cake Mix

Prep Time: 5 Minutes | Start to Finish: 5 Minutes

FOR MAKING 1 DUMP CAKE (2 CUPS)

1⅓	cups all-purpose flour
¾	cup sugar
1¼	teaspoons baking powder
¼	teaspoon salt

FOR MAKING 4 DUMP CAKES (8 CUPS)

5⅓	cups all-purpose flour
3	cups sugar
5	teaspoons baking powder
1	teaspoon salt

In medium or large bowl, mix ingredients for either 1 cake or 4 cakes until well blended. Use immediately in one of the dump cake recipes in this chapter. Or store in tightly covered container in cool, dark location up to 1 month or freeze up to 3 months.

Sweet Success Our easy master mix gives you a great head start on dessert! Make the mix for 4 cakes (which yields 8 cups) so you can store the unused portion to scoop out what you need at a moment's notice.

To make 1 dump cake with a purchased cake mix instead of this Master Mix, use half a box (15.25-ounce size) of yellow cake mix (about 1½ cups). Store the remaining cake mix in a resealable food-storage plastic bag for the next time you want to make a dump cake.

Mango-Strawberry Dump Cake

8 servings | Prep Time: 15 Minutes | Start to Finish: 55 Minutes

- 3 cups chopped fresh mangoes (1-inch pieces)
- 3 cups sliced fresh strawberries
- ⅓ cup sugar
- 1 single recipe Master Scratch Dump Cake Mix (page 76, 2 cups)
- ¾ cup butter, melted
- ½ cup sliced almonds

  Vanilla ice cream or Sweetened Whipped Cream (page 109), if desired

1 Heat oven to 350°F. Spray bottom and sides of 13x9-inch pan with cooking spray. Place mangoes and strawberries in pan. Sprinkle with sugar; stir gently to combine. Spread fruit evenly in pan.

2 Sprinkle cake mix evenly over fruit; drizzle with melted butter. Sprinkle with almonds.

3 Bake 35 to 40 minutes or until golden brown. Serve warm with ice cream or whipped cream.

1 Serving: Calories 440; Total Fat 21g (Saturated Fat 11g, Trans Fat 0.5g); Cholesterol 45mg; Sodium 290mg; Total Carbohydrate 58g (Dietary Fiber 3g); Protein 4g **Exchanges:** 1 Starch, 1½ Fruit, 1½ Other Carbohydrate, 4 Fat **Carbohydrate Choices:** 4

Sweet Success If your fruit is very ripe and sweet, reduce the sugar from ⅓ to ¼ cup.

You will need about 6 medium mangoes to get 3 cups chopped fruit. With knife, score peel lengthwise into fourths; peel the mango like a banana. Cut peeled mango flesh lengthwise close to both sides of seed; chop flesh.

Bananas Foster Dump Cake

8 servings | Prep Time: 15 Minutes | Start to Finish: 50 Minutes

⅓ cup butter

¼ cup rum or 1 tablespoon rum plus enough water to measure ¼ cup

½ cup packed brown sugar

6 cups sliced ripe bananas (about 6 medium)

1 single recipe Master Scratch Dump Cake Mix (page 76, 2 cups)

¾ cup butter, melted

¾ cup coarsely chopped pecans

Vanilla ice cream or Sweetened Whipped Cream (page 109), if desired

Caramel topping, if desired

Additional chopped pecans, if desired

1 Heat oven to 350°F. In 13x19-inch pan, melt ⅓ cup butter in oven. Stir in rum and brown sugar until well blended. Arrange bananas over brown sugar mixture.

2 Sprinkle cake mix evenly over bananas; drizzle with ¾ cup melted butter. Sprinkle with pecans.

3 Bake 30 to 35 minutes or until light golden brown. Serve warm. Top with ice cream, caramel topping and additional pecans.

1 Serving: Calories 620; Total Fat 33g (Saturated Fat 17g, Trans Fat 1g); Cholesterol 65mg; Sodium 350mg; Total Carbohydrate 75g (Dietary Fiber 4g); Protein 4g **Exchanges:** 1 Starch, 4 Other Carbohydrate, 6½ Fat **Carbohydrate Choices:** 5

Mixed Berry-Peach Dump Cake

8 servings | Prep Time: 15 Minutes | Start to Finish: 1 Hour

4 cups fresh mixed berries (blueberries, raspberries, blackberries and small strawberries)

2 cups sliced peeled peaches

⅓ cup sugar

1 single recipe Master Scratch Dump Cake Mix (page 76, 2 cups)

⅔ cup old-fashioned or quick-cooking oats

¾ cup butter, melted

Vanilla ice cream or Sweetened Whipped Cream (page 109), if desired

1 Heat oven to 350°F. Spray bottom and sides of 13x9-inch pan with cooking spray. Place berries and peaches in pan. Sprinkle with sugar; stir gently to combine. Spread fruit evenly in pan.

2 In medium bowl, stir together cake mix and oats; sprinkle evenly over fruit. Drizzle with melted butter.

3 Bake 38 to 42 minutes or until light golden brown and cake is set. Serve warm with ice cream.

1 Serving: Calories 420; Total Fat 18g (Saturated Fat 11g, Trans Fat 0.5g); Cholesterol 45mg; Sodium 290mg; Total Carbohydrate 60g (Dietary Fiber 5g); Protein 4g **Exchanges:** 1 Starch, 1 Fruit, 2 Other Carbohydrate, 3½ Fat **Carbohydrate Choices:** 4

Sweet Success Frozen mixed berries and frozen sliced peaches can be substituted for the fresh fruit; do not thaw. If frozen fruit is used, increase bake time to 40 to 45 minutes.

Rhubarb-Raspberry Dump Cake

8 servings | Prep Time: 15 Minutes | Start to Finish: 1 Hour 5 Minutes

3 cups chopped fresh rhubarb (½-inch pieces)

3 cups fresh raspberries

⅔ cup granulated sugar

1 single recipe Master Scratch Dump Cake Mix (page 76, 2 cups)

¾ cup butter, melted

1 tablespoon finely chopped crystallized ginger

1 tablespoon clear or white decorator sugar crystals

Vanilla ice cream or Sweetened Whipped Cream (page 109), if desired

1 Heat oven to 350°F. Spray bottom and sides of 13x9-inch pan with cooking spray. Place rhubarb and raspberries in pan. Sprinkle with granulated sugar; stir gently to combine. Spread fruit evenly in pan.

2 Sprinkle cake mix evenly over fruit. Drizzle with melted butter; sprinkle with ginger and sugar crystals.

3 Bake 43 to 48 minutes or until golden brown. Serve warm with ice cream.

1 Serving: Calories 430; Total Fat 18g (Saturated Fat 11g, Trans Fat 0.5g); Cholesterol 45mg; Sodium 290mg; Total Carbohydrate 63g (Dietary Fiber 4g); Protein 3g **Exchanges:** 1 Starch, 1½ Fruit, 1½ Other Carbohydrate, 3½ Fat **Carbohydrate Choices:** 4

Sweet Success Frozen rhubarb and raspberries can be substituted for fresh fruit. Thaw the rhubarb but not the raspberries. If using frozen fruit, increase bake time to 50 to 55 minutes.

Red, White and Blue Poke Cake

16 servings | Prep Time: 20 Minutes | Start to Finish: 5 Hours

1 box (16.25 oz) white cake mix with pudding in the mix

Water, vegetable oil and egg whites called for on cake mix box

1 box (4-serving size) strawberry-flavored gelatin

1 cup boiling water

½ cup cold water

1 box (4-serving size) white chocolate instant pudding and pie filling mix

⅓ cup milk

1 container (8 oz) frozen whipped topping, thawed

1 cup sliced fresh strawberries

½ cup fresh blueberries

1 Heat oven to 350°F (325°F for dark or nonstick pan). Make and bake cake mix as directed on box for 13x9-inch pan, using water, oil and egg whites. Cool completely in pan on cooling rack, about 1 hour.

2 With long-tined fork, pierce cake every ½ inch. In medium bowl, stir gelatin and boiling water until dissolved. Stir in cold water. Carefully pour mixture over entire surface of cake. Refrigerate at least 3 hours.

3 In large bowl, beat pudding mix and milk with whisk until well blended. Gently stir in whipped topping. Spread over cake. Arrange strawberries and blueberries on top of cake to look like American flag. Store loosely covered in refrigerator.

1 Serving: Calories 250; Total Fat 9g (Saturated Fat 4g, Trans Fat 0g); Cholesterol 0mg; Sodium 330mg; Total Carbohydrate 39g (Dietary Fiber 1g); Protein 3g **Exchanges:** 1 Starch, 1½ Other Carbohydrate, 1½ Fat **Carbohydrate Choices:** 2½

The Wow Factor Cut the cake into serving-size pieces and arrange on a platter. Insert a tiny American flag, available at craft stores, into each piece. Garnish the platter with whole strawberries and blueberries.

Chocolate-Peppermint Poke Cake

15 servings | Prep Time: 20 Minutes | Start to Finish: 3 Hours 10 Minutes

CAKE

1 box (15.25 oz) chocolate fudge cake mix with pudding in the mix

Water, vegetable oil and eggs called for on cake mix box

FILLING

1 box (4-serving size) white chocolate instant pudding and pie filling mix

2 cups milk

½ teaspoon peppermint extract

FROSTING

¼ teaspoon peppermint extract

1 container (12 oz) milk chocolate whipped ready-to-spread frosting

¾ cup coarsely chopped chocolate-covered peppermint patties (8 candies)

1 Heat oven to 350°F (325°F for dark or nonstick pan). Spray bottom only of 13x9-inch pan with baking spray with flour.

2 Make and bake cake mix as directed on box for 13x9-inch pan, using water, oil and eggs. Cool 15 minutes. With end of wooden spoon handle, poke top of warm cake every ½ inch.

3 In medium bowl, beat filling ingredients with whisk about 2 minutes. Immediately pour over cake. Cover loosely; refrigerate about 2 hours or until chilled.

4 Stir ¼ teaspoon peppermint extract into frosting. Frost cake; sprinkle with peppermint patties. Store covered in refrigerator.

1 Serving: Calories 360; Total Fat 15g (Saturated Fat 4.5g, Trans Fat 1g); Cholesterol 45mg; Sodium 430mg; Total Carbohydrate 52g (Dietary Fiber 1g); Protein 4g **Exchanges:** 1 Starch, 2½ Other Carbohydrate, 3 Fat **Carbohydrate Choices:** 3½

Sweet Success To keep the peppermint patties from sticking together as you chop them, sprinkle 1 tablespoon sugar over the cutting board. As you cut the candies, toss them with the sugar.

Vanilla or chocolate pudding mix can be used instead of the white chocolate pudding mix.

Chocolate Chip–Caramel Poke Cake

15 servings | Prep Time: 20 Minutes | Start to Finish: 2 Hours 35 Minutes

1 box (15.25 oz) devil's food cake mix with pudding in the mix

1¼ cups buttermilk

½ cup vegetable oil

3 eggs

2 cups semisweet chocolate chips (about 12 oz)

1 cup caramel topping

½ cup vanilla creamy ready-to-spread frosting (from 16-oz container)

1 Heat oven to 350°F (325°F for dark or nonstick pan). Spray bottom only of 13x9-inch pan with baking spray with flour.

2 In large bowl, beat cake mix, buttermilk, oil and eggs with electric mixer on low speed 30 seconds, then on medium speed 2 minutes, scraping bowl occasionally. Pour batter into pan. Sprinkle with chocolate chips; press gently into batter.

3 Bake 35 to 43 minutes or until toothpick inserted in center comes out clean. Cool 30 minutes. Spray long-tined fork with cooking spray; pierce warm cake every inch with fork. Pour caramel topping over cake. Cool completely in pan on cooling rack, about 1 hour.

4 In medium microwavable bowl, microwave frosting uncovered on High 15 to 30 seconds; stir until very soft. Spoon frosting into 1-quart resealable food-storage plastic bag; seal bag. Cut small tip off bottom corner of bag; squeeze bag to drizzle frosting across top of cake. Store covered at room temperature.

1 Serving: Calories 450; Total Fat 20g (Saturated Fat 7g, Trans Fat 1g); Cholesterol 45mg; Sodium 410mg; Total Carbohydrate 63g (Dietary Fiber 2g); Protein 5g **Exchanges:** 1 Starch, 3 Other Carbohydrate, 4 Fat **Carbohydrate Choices:** 4

Margarita Cake

15 servings | Prep Time: 20 Minutes | Start to Finish: 2 Hours

CRUST

1½   cups coarsely crushed pretzels (about 3½ cups small pretzel twists)

½   cup sugar

½   cup butter, melted

CAKE

1   box (16.25 oz) white cake mix with pudding in the mix

¾   cup bottled nonalcoholic margarita mix

½   cup water

⅓   cup vegetable oil

1   tablespoon grated lime peel

3   egg whites

TOPPING

1   container (8 oz) frozen whipped topping, thawed (3½ cups)

     Additional grated lime peel, if desired

1   Heat oven to 350°F (325°F for dark or nonstick pan). Grease bottom only of 13x9-inch pan and lightly flour, or spray with baking spray with flour. In medium bowl, mix crust ingredients. Sprinkle evenly on bottom of pan; press gently.

2   In large bowl, beat cake ingredients with electric mixer on low speed 30 seconds, then on medium speed 2 minutes, scraping bowl occasionally. Pour batter over crust.

3   Bake 34 to 39 minutes or until light golden brown and top springs back when touched lightly in center. Cool completely in pan on cooling rack, about 1 hour.

4   Spread whipped topping over cake; sprinkle with additional lime peel. Store loosely covered in refrigerator.

1 Serving: Calories 330; Total Fat 16g (Saturated Fat 8g, Trans Fat 0g); Cholesterol 15mg; Sodium 350mg; Total Carbohydrate 45g (Dietary Fiber 0g); Protein 3g **Exchanges:** 1 Starch, 2 Other Carbohydrate, 3 Fat **Carbohydrate Choices:** 3

Sweet Success Look for the bottled pale green nonalcoholic margarita mix in the soft drink section of the supermarket. It's usually on the shelf with club soda, tonic water and other mixers.

Chocolate Rum Cake

15 servings | Prep Time: 25 Minutes | Start to Finish: 4 Hours 10 Minutes

CAKE

- 1 box (15.25 oz) devil's food or dark chocolate cake mix with pudding in the mix
- 1 cup water
- ⅓ cup vegetable oil
- 3 eggs
- 1 cup whipping cream
- 1 cup whole milk
- 1 can (14 oz) sweetened condensed milk (not evaporated)
- ⅓ cup rum or 1 tablespoon rum extract plus enough water to measure ⅓ cup

TOPPING

- 1 cup whipping cream
- 2 tablespoons rum or 1 teaspoon rum extract
- ½ teaspoon vanilla
- 1 cup flaked coconut, toasted*
- ½ cup chopped pecans, toasted**

1 Heat oven to 350°F (325°F for dark or nonstick pan). Grease bottom only of 13x9-inch pan with shortening or cooking spray.

2 In large bowl, beat cake mix, water, oil and eggs with electric mixer on low speed 30 seconds, then on medium speed 2 minutes, scraping bowl occasionally. Pour batter into pan.

3 Bake 30 to 38 minutes or until toothpick inserted in center comes out clean. Cool 5 minutes.

4 With long-tined fork, pierce top of hot cake every ½ inch, wiping fork occasionally to reduce sticking. In large bowl, mix 1 cup whipping cream, the whole milk, condensed milk and ⅓ cup rum. Carefully pour mixture over top of cake. Cover; refrigerate about 3 hours or until chilled and most of whipping cream mixture has been absorbed into cake.

5 In chilled large bowl, beat 1 cup whipping cream, 2 tablespoons rum and the vanilla with electric mixer on high speed until soft peaks form. Frost cake; sprinkle with coconut and pecans. Store covered in refrigerator.

*To toast coconut, spread in ungreased shallow pan. Bake uncovered at 350°F 5 to 7 minutes, stirring occasionally, until golden brown.

**To toast pecans, spread in ungreased shallow pan. Bake uncovered at 350°F 6 to 10 minutes, stirring occasionally, until light brown.

1 Serving: Calories 430; Total Fat 24g (Saturated Fat 12g, Trans Fat 0g); Cholesterol 90mg; Sodium 330mg; Total Carbohydrate 43g (Dietary Fiber 1g); Protein 6g **Exchanges:** 1½ Starch, 1½ Other Carbohydrate, 4½ Fat **Carbohydrate Choices:** 3

Spicy Mexican Brownie Cake

15 servings | Prep Time: 30 Minutes | Start to Finish: 2 Hours 10 Minutes

CAKE

1¼	cups butter, softened
¾	cup unsweetened baking cocoa
4	eggs
2	cups granulated sugar
1½	cups all-purpose flour
1½	teaspoons baking powder
1	teaspoon ground cinnamon
¼	teaspoon plus ⅛ teaspoon ground red pepper (cayenne)
¼	teaspoon salt
½	cup milk
1	tablespoon vanilla

FROSTING

⅓	cup butter, softened
⅓	cup crema (Mexican-style cream) or sour cream
¼	teaspoon ground cinnamon
¾	teaspoon vanilla
4	cups powdered sugar
1	to 2 teaspoons milk
	Unsweetened baking cocoa, if desired

1 Heat oven to 350°F. Grease bottom and sides of 13x9-inch pan with shortening; lightly flour.

2 In small bowl, stir 1¼ cups butter and ¾ cup cocoa until blended. In large bowl, beat eggs with electric mixer on high speed 3 minutes. On low speed, beat in cocoa mixture and remaining cake ingredients just until blended. Spread batter in pan.

3 Bake 35 to 40 minutes or until top edge of cake just begins to pull away from sides of pan. (Top may appear irregular with slight dips in some spots.) Cool completely in pan on cooling rack, about 1 hour.

4 In large bowl, beat ⅓ cup butter with electric mixer on medium speed until fluffy. Beat in crema, ¼ teaspoon cinnamon and ¾ teaspoon vanilla until light and fluffy, scraping bowl frequently. On low speed, beat in powdered sugar, 1 cup at a time, scraping bowl occasionally. Stir in milk, 1 teaspoon at a time, until frosting is smooth and spreadable. Frost cake; sprinkle lightly with cocoa. Store in refrigerator.

1 Serving: Calories 510; Total Fat 23g (Saturated Fat 14g, Trans Fat 1g); Cholesterol 105mg; Sodium 290mg; Total Carbohydrate 72g (Dietary Fiber 2g); Protein 4g **Exchanges:** 1 Starch, 4 Other Carbohydrate, 4½ Fat **Carbohydrate Choices:** 5

Sweet Success Crema is a full-bodied, rich-flavored sour cream sold in a jar in the dairy case. There are two types you can buy—the "Agria" variety works well for this recipe.

Sour Cream Spice Cake

16 servings | Prep Time: 30 Minutes | Start to Finish: 2 Hours 15 Minutes

CAKE

2¼	cups all-purpose flour
1½	cups packed brown sugar
1	cup raisins, chopped
1	container (8 oz) sour cream
½	cup chopped walnuts
¼	cup butter, softened
¼	cup shortening
½	cup water
2	teaspoons ground cinnamon
1¼	teaspoons baking soda
1	teaspoon baking powder
¾	teaspoon ground cloves
½	teaspoon salt
½	teaspoon ground nutmeg
2	eggs

FROSTING

⅓	cup butter*
3	cups powdered sugar
1½	teaspoons vanilla
1	to 2 tablespoons milk
	Additional chopped walnuts, if desired

1 Heat oven to 350°F. Grease bottom and sides of 13x9-inch pan with shortening; lightly flour.

2 In large bowl, beat cake ingredients with electric mixer on low speed 30 seconds, scraping bowl constantly. Beat on high speed 3 minutes, scraping bowl occasionally. Pour batter into pan.

3 Bake 40 to 45 minutes or until toothpick inserted in center comes out clean. Cool completely in pan on cooling rack, about 1 hour.

4 Meanwhile, in 1-quart saucepan, heat ⅓ cup butter over medium heat just until light brown, stirring constantly. (Watch carefully because butter can brown and then burn quickly.) Remove from heat; cool. In medium bowl, mix powdered sugar and browned butter until well blended. Add vanilla and milk; beat until frosting is smooth and spreadable. Frost cake. Sprinkle with additional walnuts.

*Do not use margarine or vegetable oil spreads in the frosting.

1 Serving: Calories 420; Total Fat 16g (Saturated Fat 7g, Trans Fat 0g); Cholesterol 50mg; Sodium 290mg; Total Carbohydrate 65g (Dietary Fiber 1g); Protein 4g **Exchanges:** 1 Starch, 3½ Other Carbohydrate, 3 Fat **Carbohydrate Choices:** 4

Sweet Potato Cake with Maple Frosting

15 servings | Prep Time: 30 Minutes | Start to Finish: 2 Hours 10 Minutes

CAKE

2½	cups all-purpose flour
1¼	cups granulated sugar
1½	teaspoons baking soda
1	teaspoon baking powder
1	teaspoon salt
1	teaspoon ground cinnamon
1	teaspoon ground nutmeg
½	teaspoon ground cloves
1½	cups mashed cooked dark-orange sweet potatoes (2 medium)
½	cup butter, softened
½	cup buttermilk
1	teaspoon vanilla
2	eggs

FROSTING

4	cups powdered sugar
½	cup butter, softened
2	teaspoons maple flavor
3	to 4 tablespoons milk

1 Heat oven to 350°F. Grease bottom and sides of 13x9-inch pan with shortening; lightly flour.

2 In large bowl, beat cake ingredients with electric mixer on low speed, scraping bowl occasionally, until blended. Beat on high speed 3 minutes, scraping bowl occasionally. Pour batter into pan.

3 Bake 35 to 40 minutes or until golden brown and toothpick inserted in center comes out clean. Cool completely in pan on cooling rack, about 1 hour.

4 In medium bowl, beat frosting ingredients with electric mixer on low speed, adding enough milk until frosting is smooth and spreadable. Frost cake.

1 Serving: Calories 420; Total Fat 14g (Saturated Fat 8g, Trans Fat 0.5g); Cholesterol 60mg; Sodium 450mg; Total Carbohydrate 71g (Dietary Fiber 1g); Protein 4g **Exchanges:** 1½ Starch, 3 Other Carbohydrate, 2½ Fat **Carbohydrate Choices:** 5

Sweet Success It's easy to cook the sweet potatoes in the microwave. Pierce whole potatoes with a fork; place on microwavable paper towels. Microwave on High 9 to 11 minutes or until tender. Cover; let stand 5 minutes. When cool enough to handle, cut each potato lengthwise. Scoop out flesh into bowl; mash with fork. Cool before using.

The Wow Factor Look for small decorative picks at cake supply or party stores to poke into each piece of cake to highlight the theme of your party!

Take-Along Carrot Cake

12 servings | Prep Time: 30 Minutes | Start to Finish: 2 Hours 15 Minutes

CAKE

1½	cups granulated sugar
1	cup vegetable oil
3	eggs
2	cups all-purpose flour
2	teaspoons ground cinnamon
1	teaspoon baking soda
½	teaspoon salt
1	teaspoon vanilla
3	cups shredded carrots (4 medium)
1	can (8 oz) crushed pineapple in juice, drained (½ cup)
1	cup chopped nuts
½	cup coconut

FROSTING

1	package (8 oz) cream cheese, softened
¼	cup butter, softened
2	to 3 teaspoons milk
1	teaspoon vanilla
4	cups powdered sugar

1 Heat oven to 350°F. Grease bottom and sides of 13x9-inch pan with shortening; lightly flour.

2 In large bowl, beat granulated sugar, oil and eggs with electric mixer on low speed about 30 seconds or until blended. Add flour, cinnamon, baking soda, salt and 1 teaspoon vanilla; beat on medium speed 1 minute. Stir in carrots, pineapple, nuts and coconut (batter will be thick). Spread batter in pan.

3 Bake 40 to 45 minutes or until toothpick inserted in center comes out clean. Cool completely in pan on cooling rack, about 1 hour.

4 In large bowl, beat cream cheese, butter, milk and 1 teaspoon vanilla with electric mixer on low speed until smooth. Gradually beat in powdered sugar, 1 cup at a time, until frosting is smooth and spreadable. Frost cake. Store covered in refrigerator.

1 Serving: Calories 730; Total Fat 38g (Saturated Fat 11g, Trans Fat 0g); Cholesterol 80mg; Sodium 350mg; Total Carbohydrate 90g (Dietary Fiber 2g); Protein 7g **Exchanges:** 1 Starch, 5 Other Carbohydrate, ½ Vegetable, ½ Very Lean Meat, 7½ Fat **Carbohydrate Choices:** 6

Apple Cake Substitute 3 cups chopped peeled tart apples (3 medium) for the carrots.

Zucchini Cake Substitute 3 cups shredded zucchini (2 to 3 medium) for the carrots.

Raspberry-Lemonade Cake

12 servings | Prep Time: 25 Minutes | Start to Finish: 2 Hours

CAKE AND FILLING

- 1 cup very hot water
- 1 box (4-serving size) raspberry-flavored gelatin
- 1 box (16.25 oz) white cake mix with pudding in the mix
- ½ cup frozen (thawed) lemonade concentrate
- ¼ cup water
- ⅓ cup vegetable oil
- 4 egg whites

FROSTING AND DECORATIONS

- 1 container (12 oz) vanilla whipped ready-to-spread frosting
- 1 cup frozen (thawed) whipped topping
- 1½ cups fresh raspberries, if desired

  Lemon peel strips, if desired

1 Heat oven to 350°F (325°F for dark or nonstick pan). Spray bottom only of 1 (13x9-inch) pan with baking spray with flour. In small bowl, mix hot water and gelatin until gelatin is completely dissolved; cool slightly.

2 In large bowl, beat cake mix, ¼ cup of the gelatin mixture, ¼ cup of the lemonade concentrate, the water, oil and egg whites with electric mixer on low speed 30 seconds, then on medium speed 2 minutes. Pour batter into pan. Reserve remaining gelatin mixture and lemonade concentrate.

3 Bake 25 to 31 minutes or until toothpick inserted in center comes out clean. With long-tined fork, pierce top of warm cake every inch. Remove 1 tablespoon of the reserved gelatin mixture to microwavable custard cup or small bowl. In another small bowl, mix remaining gelatin mixture and remaining ¼ cup lemonade concentrate; pour slowly over cake. Cool completely, about 1 hour.

4 In medium bowl, fold together frosting and whipped topping. Frost cake. Microwave 1 tablespoon gelatin mixture uncovered on High 10 seconds to liquefy. Using ¼ teaspoon measuring spoon, place small drops of gelatin mixture over frosting. Using spoon or toothpick, swirl gelatin into frosting. Top each piece with raspberries and lemon peel. Store covered in refrigerator.

1 Serving: Calories 400; Total Fat 15g (Saturated Fat 4.5g, Trans Fat 2g); Cholesterol 0mg; Sodium 350mg; Total Carbohydrate 62g (Dietary Fiber 0g); Protein 3g **Exchanges:** 1 Starch, 3 Other Carbohydrate, 3 Fat **Carbohydrate Choices:** 4

Sweet Success To make the lemon peel strips for the garnish, use a carrot peeler or small knife. Be sure to cut just the yellow peel and not the white pith under it.

If you plan to tote this cake to a get-together, be sure to use an insulated cooler to keep it cold.

The Wow Factor For a shower dessert, garnish each piece with a small paper beverage umbrella.

Lemonade Party Cake

12 servings | Prep Time: 15 Minutes | Start to Finish: 3 Hours

CAKE

1   box (15.25 oz) lemon or yellow cake mix with pudding in the mix

     Water, vegetable oil and eggs called for on cake mix box

1   can (6 oz) frozen lemonade concentrate, thawed

¾   cup powdered sugar

FROSTING

1   container (16 oz) lemon creamy ready-to-spread frosting

1 Heat oven to 350°F (325°F for dark or nonstick pan). Grease bottom only of 13x9-inch pan with shortening or cooking spray.

2 Make and bake cake mix as directed on box for 13x9-inch pan, using water, oil and eggs. Cool 15 minutes.

3 With long-tined fork, pierce top of warm cake every ½ inch, wiping fork occasionally to reduce sticking. In small bowl, mix lemonade concentrate and powdered sugar. Drizzle mixture over top of cake. Run knife around sides of pan to loosen cake. Cover; refrigerate about 2 hours or until chilled.

4 Frost cake with lemon frosting; sprinkle with yellow sugar. Garnish individual servings with lemon slice and mint leaf. Store covered in refrigerator.

1 Serving: Calories 410; Total Fat 18g (Saturated Fat 4.5g, Trans Fat 2g); Cholesterol 55mg; Sodium 310mg; Total Carbohydrate 62g (Dietary Fiber 0g); Protein 2g **Exchanges:** 1 Starch, 3 Other Carbohydrate, 3½ Fat **Carbohydrate Choices:** 4

Cherry-Chocolate Chip Cake

15 servings | Prep Time: 20 Minutes | Start to Finish: 2 Hours

1 cup miniature semisweet chocolate chips

1 box (16.25 oz) white cake mix with pudding in the mix

¾ cup water

½ cup sour cream

⅓ cup vegetable oil

1 teaspoon almond extract

4 egg whites

2 jars (10 oz each) maraschino cherries, well drained, chopped (1 cup)

1 container (16 oz) cherry creamy ready-to-spread frosting

1 Heat oven to 350°F (325°F for dark or nonstick pan). Generously grease bottom only of 13x9-inch pan and lightly flour, or spray with baking spray with flour.

2 In small bowl, coat chocolate chips in 1 tablespoon cake mix; set aside. In large bowl, beat remaining cake mix, the water, sour cream, oil, almond extract and egg whites with electric mixer on low speed 30 seconds. Beat on medium speed 2 minutes.

3 Drain chopped cherries on paper towels; pat dry. Stir cherries and reserved chocolate chips into batter. Pour batter into pan.

4 Bake 31 to 37 minutes or until cake springs back when touched lightly in center. Run knife around side of pan to loosen cake. Cool completely in pan on cooling rack, about 1 hour. Frost cake with cherry frosting. Store loosely covered.

1 Serving: Calories 380; Total Fat 15g (Saturated Fat 5g, Trans Fat 2g); Cholesterol 0mg; Sodium 300mg; Total Carbohydrate 57g (Dietary Fiber 1g); Protein 3g **Exchanges:** 1 Starch, 3 Other Carbohydrate, 3 Fat **Carbohydrate Choices:** 4

Lemon Buttermilk Sheet Cake

24 servings | Prep Time: 15 Minutes | Start to Finish: 1 Hour 40 Minutes

CAKE

1   box (15.25 oz) lemon cake mix with pudding in the mix

1   cup buttermilk

½   cup vegetable oil

3   eggs

FROSTING

⅓   cup shortening

⅓   cup butter, softened

1   teaspoon grated lemon peel

2   tablespoons lemon juice

3   cups powdered sugar

1 Heat oven to 350°F (325°F for dark or nonstick pan). Spray bottom and sides of 15x10x1-inch jelly roll pan with baking spray with flour.

2 In large bowl, beat cake ingredients with electric mixer on low speed 30 seconds, then on medium speed 2 minutes, scraping bowl occasionally. Pour batter into pan.

3 Bake 20 to 25 minutes or until toothpick inserted in center comes out clean or cake springs back when touched lightly in center. Cool completely in pan on cooling rack, about 1 hour.

4 In medium bowl, beat frosting ingredients with electric mixer on high speed until smooth and creamy (add more lemon juice if needed). Frost cake. Store loosely covered.

1 Serving: Calories 230; Total Fat 11g (Saturated Fat 4g, Trans Fat 0.5g); Cholesterol 35mg; Sodium 170mg; Total Carbohydrate 31g (Dietary Fiber 0g); Protein 1g **Exchanges:** ½ Starch, 1½ Other Carbohydrate, 2 Fat **Carbohydrate Choices:** 2

The Wow Factor For a large group, cut the cake into 48 small squares and serve in small, colorful paper baking cups.

Banana Tres Leches Cake

16 servings | Prep Time: 20 Minutes | Start to Finish: 4 Hours

1   box (16.25 oz) white cake mix
     with pudding in the mix

1¼   cups water

2   tablespoons vegetable oil

3   eggs

1   cup mashed bananas
     (2 medium)

1   can (14 oz) sweetened
     condensed milk
     (not evaporated)

½   cup canned coconut milk
     (not cream of coconut)

½   cup whipping cream

1   container (12 oz)
     fluffy white whipped
     ready-to-spread frosting

     Banana slices, if desired

     Toasted coconut*, if desired

1 Heat oven to 350°F (325°F for dark or nonstick pan). Grease bottom only of 13x9-inch pan with shortening or cooking spray.

2 In large bowl, beat cake mix, water, oil, eggs and mashed bananas with electric mixer on low speed 30 seconds, then on medium speed 2 minutes, scraping bowl occasionally. Pour batter into pan.

3 Bake 33 to 38 minutes or until toothpick inserted in center comes out clean. Cool completely in pan on cooling rack, about 1 hour.

4 With long-tined fork, pierce top of cake every ½ inch, wiping fork occasionally to reduce sticking. In large bowl, stir together condensed milk, coconut milk and whipping cream. Carefully pour milk mixture evenly over top of cake. Cover; refrigerate at least 2 hours or overnight until mixture is absorbed into cake.

5 Frost cake with frosting. Garnish individual servings with banana slices and toasted coconut. Store loosely covered in refrigerator.

*To toast coconut, spread in ungreased shallow pan. Bake uncovered at 350°F 5 to 7 minutes, stirring occasionally, until golden brown.

1 Serving: Calories 360; Total Fat 14g (Saturated Fat 7g, Trans Fat 1.5g); Cholesterol 50mg; Sodium 280mg; Total Carbohydrate 54g (Dietary Fiber 0g); Protein 4g **Exchanges:** 1 Starch, 2½ Other Carbohydrate, 2½ Fat **Carbohydrate Choices:** 3½

Betty Crocker Sheet Pan Desserts

Easy Pineapple Upside-Down Cake

12 servings | Prep Time: 10 Minutes | Start to Finish: 1 Hour 35 Minutes

¼ cup butter

1 cup packed brown sugar

1 can (20 oz) pineapple slices in juice, drained, juice reserved

1 jar (6 oz) maraschino cherries without stems, drained

1 box (15.25 oz) yellow cake mix with pudding in the mix

Vegetable oil and eggs called for on cake mix box

Sweetened Whipped Cream (page 109), if desired

1 Heat oven to 350°F (325°F for dark or nonstick pan). In 13x9-inch pan, melt butter in oven. Sprinkle brown sugar evenly over butter. Arrange pineapple slices on brown sugar. Place cherry in center of each pineapple slice, and arrange remaining cherries around slices; press gently into brown sugar.

2 Add enough water to reserved pineapple juice to measure 1 cup. Make cake batter as directed on box, using oil and eggs and substituting pineapple juice mixture for the water. Pour batter over pineapple and cherries.

3 Bake 42 to 48 minutes or until toothpick inserted in center comes out clean. Immediately run knife around sides of pan to loosen cake. Place heatproof serving plate upside down over pan; turn plate and pan over. Let stand 5 minutes so topping drizzles over cake; remove pan. Cool 30 minutes. Serve warm or cool with whipped cream. Store covered in refrigerator.

1 Serving: Calories 390; Total Fat 16g (Saturated Fat 5g, Trans Fat 0g); Cholesterol 65mg; Sodium 310mg; Total Carbohydrate 60g (Dietary Fiber 1g); Protein 2g **Exchanges:** ½ Starch, 3½ Other Carbohydrate, 3 Fat **Carbohydrate Choices:** 4

Sweetened Whipped Cream

For 3 cups of sweetened whipped cream, in chilled large bowl, beat 1½ cups whipping cream, 3 tablespoons granulated or powdered sugar and 1½ teaspoons vanilla with electric mixer on low speed until mixture begins to thicken. Gradually increase speed to high and beat just until soft peaks form.

Strawberry-Rhubarb Upside-Down Cake

12 servings | Prep Time: 20 Minutes | Start to Finish: 1 Hour 50 Minutes

¼ cup butter

1 cup packed brown sugar

2 cups sliced fresh strawberries

2 cups chopped fresh rhubarb

1 box (15.25 oz) French vanilla or yellow cake mix with pudding in the mix

1 cup water

⅓ cup vegetable oil

3 eggs

Sweetened Whipped Cream (page 109), if desired

1 Heat oven to 350°F (325°F for dark or nonstick pan). In 13x9-inch pan, melt butter in oven. Sprinkle brown sugar evenly over butter. Arrange strawberries on brown sugar; sprinkle evenly with rhubarb. Press strawberries and rhubarb gently into brown sugar.

2 In large bowl, beat cake mix, water, oil and eggs with electric mixer on low speed 30 seconds, then on medium speed 2 minutes, scraping bowl occasionally. Pour batter over strawberries and rhubarb.

3 Bake 46 to 52 minutes or until toothpick inserted in center comes out clean. Immediately run knife around sides of pan to loosen cake. Place heatproof serving plate upside down over pan; turn plate and pan over. Let stand 5 minutes so topping drizzles over cake. Cool 30 minutes. Serve warm or cool with whipped cream. Store covered in refrigerator.

1 Serving: Calories 330; Total Fat 13g (Saturated Fat 4.5g, Trans Fat 0g); Cholesterol 65mg; Sodium 310mg; Total Carbohydrate 50g (Dietary Fiber 1g); Protein 3g **Exchanges:** 1 Starch, ½ Fruit, 2 Other Carbohydrate, 2½ Fat **Carbohydrate Choices:** 3

Sweet Success If fresh rhubarb is out of season, use frozen rhubarb. Just thaw and drain it before making the cake.

Coffee-Toffee Cake with Caramel Frosting

15 servings | Prep Time: 15 Minutes | Start to Finish: 2 Hours

¼ cup instant coffee granules or crystals

¼ cup boiling water

1 box (16.25 oz) white cake mix with pudding in the mix

1 cup water

⅓ cup vegetable oil

3 eggs

1 container (16 oz) vanilla creamy ready-to-spread frosting

¼ cup caramel topping

3 bars (1.4 oz each) chocolate-covered English toffee candy, coarsely chopped

1 Heat oven to 350°F (325°F for dark or nonstick pan). Grease bottom and sides of 13x9-inch pan with shortening or cooking spray. In small bowl, dissolve coffee granules in boiling water.

2 In large bowl, beat cake mix, 1 cup water, the oil, eggs and coffee mixture with electric mixer on low speed 30 seconds, then on medium speed 2 minutes, scraping bowl occasionally. Pour batter into pan.

3 Bake 40 to 45 minutes or until toothpick inserted in center comes out clean or cake springs back when touched lightly in center. Cool completely in pan on cooling rack, about 1 hour.

4 In medium bowl, mix frosting and caramel topping. Frost cake. Sprinkle with toffee candy. Store loosely covered.

1 Serving: Calories 390; Total Fat 18g (Saturated Fat 5g, Trans Fat 3g); Cholesterol 45mg; Sodium 360mg; Total Carbohydrate 55g (Dietary Fiber 0g); Protein 3g **Exchanges:** 1 Starch, 2½ Other Carbohydrate, 3½ Fat **Carbohydrate Choices:** 3½

Sweet Success For an Irish cream cake, substitute ¼ cup Irish cream liqueur for the caramel topping.

Caramel Latte Cake

16 servings | Prep Time: 30 Minutes | Start to Finish: 3 Hours 20 Minutes

CAKE

- 1 box (15.25. oz) butter recipe yellow cake mix with pudding in the mix
- 1 cup warm water
- 1 tablespoon instant espresso coffee powder or granules
- ⅓ cup butter, melted
- 3 eggs

FILLING

- 1 can (13.4 oz) dulce de leche (caramelized sweetened condensed milk)
- ½ cup hot water
- 3 tablespoons instant espresso coffee powder or granules
- 1 tablespoon dark rum or 1 teaspoon rum extract plus 2 teaspoons water

FROSTING AND GARNISH

- 1 cup whipping cream
- ¼ cup powdered sugar
- 2 oz semisweet baking chocolate, grated, or 1 teaspoon unsweetened baking cocoa

1 Heat oven to 350°F (325°F for dark or nonstick pan). Spray bottom only of 13x9-inch pan with baking spray with flour.

2 In large bowl, place cake mix. In 1-cup glass measuring cup, stir 1 cup warm water and 1 tablespoon espresso powder until dissolved. Add espresso mixture, butter and eggs to cake mix. Beat with electric mixer on low speed 30 seconds, then on medium speed 2 minutes, scraping bowl occasionally. Pour batter into pan.

3 Bake 30 to 35 minutes or until toothpick inserted in center comes out clean. Cool 15 minutes.

4 Meanwhile, spoon dulce de leche into medium microwavable bowl. In small bowl, mix ½ cup hot water, 3 tablespoons espresso powder and the rum; stir into dulce de leche until smooth. Microwave uncovered on High 2 to 3 minutes, stirring after about 1 minute with whisk, until pourable.

5 With end of wooden spoon handle, poke cake every ½ inch. Pour dulce de leche mixture evenly over cake; spread with spatula to fill holes. Run knife around sides of pan to loosen cake. Cover; refrigerate 2 hours.

6 In medium bowl, beat whipping cream and powdered sugar with electric mixer on high speed until stiff peaks form. Spread whipped cream over cake. Sprinkle with grated chocolate. Store covered in refrigerator.

1 Serving: Calories 310; Total Fat 14g (Saturated Fat 9g, Trans Fat 0g); Cholesterol 75mg; Sodium 260mg; Total Carbohydrate 41g (Dietary Fiber 1g); Protein 4g **Exchanges:** 1½ Starch, 1 Other Carbohydrate, 2½ Fat **Carbohydrate Choices:** 3

Sweet Success If garnishing with cocoa, place the cocoa in a tea strainer and lightly shake over the frosting to "dust" the top of the cake.

CHAPTER THREE

Bars and Cookie Bars

Chocolate Truffle–Topped Caramel Bars

75 bars | Prep Time: 45 Minutes | Start to Finish: 3 Hours 55 Minutes

TOPPING

- ⅓ cup whipping cream
- 3 tablespoons butter
- 1 tablespoon light corn syrup
- 2 cups dark chocolate chips (about 12 oz)

CRUST

- 1 cup all-purpose flour
- ½ cup packed brown sugar
- ½ cup cold butter
- 1 cup quick-cooking or old-fashioned oats
- 1 cup chopped pecans

CARAMEL LAYER

- 1 cup butter
- 1 cup packed brown sugar
- ¼ cup light corn syrup
- ¼ teaspoon salt
- 1 can (14 oz) sweetened condensed milk (not evaporated)

1 Heat oven to 350°F. In 1-quart saucepan, heat whipping cream, 3 tablespoons butter and 1 tablespoon corn syrup to a full boil over medium heat. Remove from heat. Add chocolate chips; let stand 5 minutes without stirring, then stir slowly with whisk until chips are melted and mixture is smooth and glossy. Set aside.

2 In large bowl, stir together flour and ½ cup brown sugar. Cut in ½ cup butter, using pastry blender or fork, until mixture looks like coarse crumbs. Stir in oats and pecans. Press mixture into ungreased 15x10x1-inch jelly roll pan. Bake 15 to 20 minutes or until crust is golden brown.

3 Meanwhile, in 2-quart saucepan, heat 1 cup butter, 1 cup brown sugar, ¼ cup corn syrup, the salt and condensed milk to boiling over medium heat, stirring constantly. Boil 5 minutes, stirring constantly. Pour and spread over crust. Cool slightly, about 10 minutes.

4 Pour chocolate truffle topping over caramel layer; spread evenly. Cool in pan on cooling rack 1 hour. Refrigerate at least 2 hours before serving. Cut into 15 rows by 5 rows. Store covered in refrigerator.

1 Bar: Calories 120; Total Fat 7g (Saturated Fat 4g, Trans Fat 0g); Cholesterol 15mg; Sodium 50mg; Total Carbohydrate 13g (Dietary Fiber 0g); Protein 1g **Exchanges:** 1 Other Carbohydrate, 1½ Fat **Carbohydrate Choices:** 1

Betty Crocker Sheet Pan Desserts

Warm Toasted Marshmallow S'more Bars

24 bars | Prep Time: 20 Minutes | Start to Finish: 55 Minutes

1 pouch (1 lb 1.5 oz) sugar cookie mix

1 cup graham cracker crumbs

1 cup butter or margarine, melted

3 cups milk chocolate chips (18 oz)

4½ cups miniature marshmallows

1 Heat oven to 375°F. In large bowl, stir together cookie mix and crumbs. Stir in melted butter until soft dough forms. Press into ungreased 13x9-inch pan.

2 Bake 18 to 20 minutes or until set. Immediately sprinkle chocolate chips over crust. Let stand 3 to 5 minutes or until chocolate begins to melt. Spread chocolate evenly over crust.

3 Set oven control to broil. Sprinkle marshmallows over melted chocolate. Broil bars with top 5 to 6 inches from heat 20 to 30 seconds or until marshmallows are toasted. Cool 10 minutes. For bars, cut into 6 rows by 4 rows. Serve warm. Store any remaining bars tightly covered.

1 Bar: Calories 310; Total Fat 16g (Saturated Fat 8g, Trans Fat 1.5g); Cholesterol 25mg; Sodium 150mg; Total Carbohydrate 39g (Dietary Fiber 0g); Protein 3g **Exchanges:** 1 Starch, 1½ Other Carbohydrate, ½ High-Fat Meat, 3 Fat **Carbohydrate Choices:** 2½

No-Bake Chocolate-Peanut Butter Candy Bars

32 bars | Prep Time: 15 Minutes | Start to Finish: 45 Minutes

24	creme-filled chocolate sandwich cookies
4	cups miniature marshmallows
¼	cup butter
1	cup semisweet chocolate chips
1	can (14 oz) sweetened condensed milk (not evaporated)
1⅔	cups peanut butter chips
¼	cup creamy peanut butter
1	cup coarsely chopped honey-roasted peanuts
4	peanut butter crunchy granola bars (2 pouches from 8.9-oz box), crushed
1	teaspoon vegetable oil

1. Line 13x9-inch pan with foil, leaving foil overhanging at 2 opposite sides of pan. In food processor, process cookies until finely chopped; set aside.

2. In 2-quart saucepan, heat marshmallows and butter over low heat, stirring constantly, until melted and smooth. Stir in chopped cookies and ¾ cup of the chocolate chips until well mixed. Press in bottom of pan.

3. In medium microwavable bowl, microwave condensed milk and peanut butter chips uncovered on High 60 seconds, stirring once, until smooth. Stir in peanut butter. Stir in peanuts and crushed granola bars. Spread over chocolate layer.

4. In small microwavable bowl, microwave remaining ¼ cup chocolate chips and the oil uncovered on High 30 seconds or until chips are softened and can be stirred smooth. Drizzle chocolate diagonally over peanut butter layer.

5. Refrigerate 30 minutes or until set. Use foil to lift bars from pan. Cut into 8 rows by 4 rows.

1 Bar: Calories 240; Total Fat 12g (Saturated Fat 4g, Trans Fat 0g); Cholesterol 10mg; Sodium 130mg; Total Carbohydrate 29g (Dietary Fiber 1g); Protein 5g **Exchanges:** 2 Starch, 2 Fat **Carbohydrate Choices:** 2

Sweet Success To easily crush granola bars, leave them in the pouches. Gently pound with meat mallet or rolling pin to break them up.

Peanut-Buttery Fudge Bars

24 bars | Prep Time: 20 Minutes | Start to Finish: 3 Hours 5 Minutes

COOKIE BASE

- 1 pouch (1 lb 1.5 oz) peanut butter cookie mix
- 3 tablespoons vegetable oil
- 1 tablespoon water
- 1 egg

TOPPING

- 1 cup hot fudge topping
- 1 cup cream cheese creamy ready-to-spread frosting (from 16-oz container)
- ¼ cup creamy peanut butter
- 1 container (8 oz) frozen whipped topping, thawed (3½ cups)
- 2 bars (2.1 oz each) chocolate-covered crispy peanut-buttery candy, unwrapped, finely crushed

    Additional chocolate-covered candy, coarsely crushed, if desired

1 Heat oven to 350°F. Spray bottom only of 13x9-inch pan with cooking spray.

2 In large bowl, stir cookie mix, oil, water and egg until soft dough forms. Press dough in bottom of pan.

3 Bake 12 to 15 minutes or until light golden brown. Cool completely on cooling rack, about 30 minutes.

4 Spread fudge topping over cooled cookie base. In medium bowl, mix frosting and peanut butter. Gently fold in whipped topping and crushed candy until well blended. Spoon mixture over fudge topping and carefully spread to cover. Refrigerate about 2 hours or until chilled.

5 Sprinkle with additional chocolate-covered candy. Cut into 6 rows by 4 rows. Store covered in refrigerator.

1 Bar: Calories 260; Total Fat 12g (Saturated Fat 4g, Trans Fat 0.5g); Cholesterol 10mg; Sodium 200mg; Total Carbohydrate 36g (Dietary Fiber 0g); Protein 3g **Exchanges:** 1 Starch, 1½ Other Carbohydrate, 2 Fat **Carbohydrate Choices:** 2½

Gluten-Free Rocky Road Bars

24 bars | Prep Time: 15 Minutes | Start to Finish: 1 Hour 30 Minutes

½   cup butter, softened

1   teaspoon gluten-free vanilla

1   egg

1   box (19 oz) gluten-free chocolate chip cookie mix

2   cups semisweet chocolate chips (about 12 oz)

½   cup chopped pecans, toasted*

3   cups miniature marshmallows

1 Heat oven to 350°F. Spray bottom only of 13x9-inch pan with cooking spray (without flour).

2 In large bowl, mix butter, vanilla and egg until blended. Stir in cookie mix until soft dough forms. Press dough in bottom of pan.

3 Bake 20 to 25 minutes or until top is golden brown and center puffs slightly. Immediately sprinkle chocolate chips over hot crust. Let stand 3 to 5 minutes or until chocolate begins to melt; gently spread chocolate over crust.

4 Set oven control to broil. Sprinkle pecans and marshmallows over melted chocolate. Broil with top 5 to 6 inches from heat 20 to 30 seconds or until marshmallows are toasted. (Watch closely; marshmallows will brown quickly.) Cool 30 to 45 minutes on cooling rack to serve warm, or cool completely, about 2 hours. Cut into 6 rows by 4 rows. Store tightly covered.

*To toast pecans, spread in ungreased shallow pan. Bake uncovered at 350°F 6 to 10 minutes, stirring occasionally, until light brown.

1 Bar: Calories 250; Total Fat 12g (Saturated Fat 6g, Trans Fat 0g); Cholesterol 20mg; Sodium 140mg; Total Carbohydrate 33g (Dietary Fiber 1g); Protein 2g **Exchanges:** ½ Starch, 1½ Other Carbohydrate, 2½ Fat **Carbohydrate Choices:** 2

Sweet Success These bars are yummy served warm but are definitely "ooey-gooey," so it's best to serve them on a plate with a fork.

Cooking Gluten Free? Always read labels to make sure each recipe ingredient is gluten free. Products and ingredient sources can change.

Gluten-Free Peanut Butter–Caramel Bars

36 bars | Prep Time: 30 Minutes | Start to Finish: 2 Hours 35 Minutes

COOKIE BASE

1 box (19 oz) gluten-free chocolate chip cookie mix

Butter, gluten-free vanilla and egg called for on cookie mix box

FILLING

⅓ cup light corn syrup

3 tablespoons butter, softened

3 tablespoons peanut butter

4½ teaspoons water

1¼ teaspoons gluten-free vanilla

Dash salt

3½ cups powdered sugar

CARAMEL LAYER

1 bag (14 oz) gluten-free caramels, unwrapped

2 tablespoons water

1½ cups dry-roasted peanuts

TOPPING

2 cups milk chocolate chips (about 12 oz)

1 Heat oven to 350°F. Make cookie dough as directed on box, using butter, vanilla and egg. Press dough in bottom of ungreased 13x9-inch pan.

2 Bake 18 to 20 minutes or until light golden brown. Cool completely on cooling rack, about 30 minutes.

3 In large bowl, beat all filling ingredients except powdered sugar with electric mixer on medium speed until creamy and smooth. Gradually beat in powdered sugar until well blended (filling will be thick). Press filling over cooled baked base.

4 In medium microwavable bowl, microwave caramels and 2 tablespoons water uncovered on High 2 to 4 minutes, stirring twice, until caramels are melted. Stir in peanuts. Spread evenly over filling. Refrigerate about 15 minutes or until caramel layer is firm.

5 In small microwavable bowl, microwave chocolate chips uncovered on High 1 to 2 minutes, stirring once, until melted. Spread evenly over caramel layer.

6 Refrigerate about 1 hour or until chocolate is set. Cut into 6 rows by 6 rows. Store covered at room temperature.

1 Bar: Calories 290; Total Fat 12g (Saturated Fat 5g, Trans Fat 0g); Cholesterol 20mg; Sodium 140mg; Total Carbohydrate 42g (Dietary Fiber 1g); Protein 3g **Exchanges:** ½ Starch, 2½ Other Carbohydrate, 2½ Fat **Carbohydrate Choices:** 3

Sweet Success Powdered sugar is usually gluten free since it's blended with cornstarch to keep it fluffy. However, some manufacturers use wheat products instead of cornstarch, so always check the label when purchasing.

Cooking Gluten Free? Always read labels to make sure each recipe ingredient is gluten free. Products and ingredient sources can change.

Chocolate Chex™ Caramel Corn Bars

32 bars | Prep Time: 10 Minutes | Start to Finish: 40 Minutes

4 cups popped light butter-flavored microwave popcorn

4 cups Chocolate Chex cereal

1 cup pretzel sticks, coarsely broken

½ cup packed brown sugar

½ cup light corn syrup

⅓ cup butter

¼ cup semisweet chocolate chips

1 Butter bottom and sides of 13x9-inch pan. Remove and discard unpopped kernels from popped popcorn. In large bowl, mix popcorn, cereal and pretzels; set aside.

2 In 2-cup microwavable measuring cup, microwave brown sugar, corn syrup and butter uncovered on High 1 to 2 minutes, stirring after 1 minute, until boiling. Microwave 30 seconds longer; stir. Pour over popcorn mixture; stir until evenly coated. Press mixture firmly in pan.

3 In small microwavable bowl, microwave chocolate chips uncovered on High 30 seconds to 1 minute, stirring once, until softened and chips can be stirred smooth. Drizzle melted chocolate over bars. Cool completely in pan on cooling rack, about 30 minutes. Cut into 8 rows by 4 rows.

1 Bar: Calories 80; Total Fat 3g (Saturated Fat 1.5g, Trans Fat 0g); Cholesterol 5mg; Sodium 70mg; Total Carbohydrate 13g (Dietary Fiber 0g); Protein 0g **Exchanges:** 1 Other Carbohydrate, ½ Fat **Carbohydrate Choices:** 1

Sweet Success Spray your knife with cooking spray before cutting the bars—you'll be able to cut through the bars without the knife sticking.

Black Forest Dream Bars

20 bars | Prep Time: 15 Minutes | Start to Finish: 3 Hours 55 Minutes

1 pouch (1 lb 1.5 oz) double chocolate chunk cookie mix

¼ cup vegetable oil

1 egg

1 can (21 oz) cherry pie filling

2 packages (8 oz each) cream cheese, softened

½ cup sugar

1 container (8 oz) frozen whipped topping, thawed (3½ cups)

1 Heat oven to 350°F. In large bowl, stir cookie mix, oil and egg until soft dough forms. On ungreased cookie sheet, drop 3 tablespoonfuls of dough 2 inches apart. Bake 12 to 13 minutes or until set. Cool 2 minutes; remove from cookie sheet to cooling rack. Cool completely, about 15 minutes.

2 Lightly spray bottom and sides of 13x9-inch pan with cooking spray; press remaining dough in bottom of pan. Reserve 1 cup cherry pie filling for topping; cover with plastic wrap and refrigerate.

3 In large bowl, beat cream cheese, sugar and remaining pie filling with electric mixer on medium speed until blended. Spread cream cheese mixture over crust in pan.

4 Bake 35 to 40 minutes or until set. Cool in pan on cooling rack 30 minutes. Refrigerate about 1 hour or until chilled.

5 Spread whipped topping over cream cheese layer. Top with spoonfuls of reserved cherry pie filling. Coarsely crumble baked cookies; sprinkle over bars. Refrigerate at least 1 hour. Cut into 5 rows by 4 rows. Store covered in refrigerator.

1 Bar: Calories 320; Total Fat 15g (Saturated Fat 8g, Trans Fat 0g); Cholesterol 35mg; Sodium 190mg; Total Carbohydrate 43g (Dietary Fiber 0g); Protein 3g
Exchanges: ½ Starch, 2½ Other Carbohydrate, 3 Fat **Carbohydrate Choices:** 3

Toffee-Pecan Bars

48 bars | Prep Time: 30 Minutes | Start to Finish: 2 Hours

CRUST

- ¾ cup butter, softened
- ⅓ cup packed brown sugar
- 1 egg
- 2 cups all-purpose flour

FILLING

- 1 cup butter
- ¾ cup packed brown sugar
- ¼ cup light corn syrup
- 2 cups coarsely chopped pecans
- 1 cup swirled milk chocolate and caramel chips (from 10-oz bag)

1 Heat oven to 375°F. Grease bottom and sides of 15x10x1-inch jelly roll pan with shortening or cooking spray (do not use dark pan).

2 In large bowl, beat ¾ cup butter and ⅓ cup brown sugar with electric mixer on medium speed until light and fluffy. Add egg; beat until well blended. On low speed, beat in flour until dough begins to form. Press dough in bottom of pan.

3 Bake 12 to 17 minutes or until edges are light golden brown. Meanwhile, in 2-quart saucepan, heat 1 cup butter, ¾ cup brown sugar and the corn syrup to boiling over medium heat, stirring frequently. Boil 2 minutes without stirring.

4 Quickly stir pecans into corn syrup mixture; spread over partially baked crust. Bake 20 to 23 minutes or until filling is golden brown and bubbly.

5 Immediately sprinkle chocolate chips over hot bars. Let stand 5 minutes to soften. With rubber spatula, gently swirl melted chips over bars. Cool completely in pan on cooling rack, about 1 hour. Cut into 6 rows by 4 rows, then cut each square diagonally in half. Store covered in refrigerator.

1 Bar: Calories 160; Total Fat 11g (Saturated Fat 5g, Trans Fat 0g); Cholesterol 20mg; Sodium 50mg; Total Carbohydrate 14g (Dietary Fiber 0g); Protein 1g **Exchanges:** ½ Starch, ½ Other Carbohydrate, 2 Fat **Carbohydrate Choices:** 1

Sweet Success Coarsely chopped walnuts can be used instead of the pecans.

Toffee Bars

32 bars | Prep Time: 15 Minutes | Start to Finish: 1 Hour 20 Minutes

1 cup butter, softened
1 cup packed brown sugar
1 teaspoon vanilla
1 egg yolk
2 cups all-purpose flour
¼ teaspoon salt
⅔ cup milk chocolate chips or 3 bars (1.55 oz each) milk chocolate, chopped
½ cup chopped nuts

1 Heat oven to 350°F. In large bowl, stir butter, brown sugar, vanilla and egg yolk until well mixed. Stir in flour and salt (dough will be stiff). Press dough in bottom of ungreased 13x9-inch pan.

2 Bake 25 to 30 minutes or until very light brown (crust will be soft, do not overbake).

3 Immediately sprinkle chocolate chips over hot crust. Let stand about 5 minutes or until chips are soft; spread chocolate evenly over crust. Sprinkle with nuts. Cool 30 minutes in pan on cooling rack. For easiest cutting, cut into 8 rows by 4 rows while warm.

1 Bar: Calories 140; Total Fat 8g (Saturated Fat 4.5g, Trans Fat 0g); Cholesterol 20mg; Sodium 80mg; Total Carbohydrate 15g (Dietary Fiber 0g); Protein 1g **Exchanges:** ½ Starch, ½ Other Carbohydrate, 1½ Fat **Carbohydrate Choices:** 1

Sweet Success For even more toffee flavor, stir in ½ cup toffee bits with the flour and salt.

Quick Praline Bars

24 bars | Prep Time: 10 Minutes | Start to Finish: 25 Minutes

24 graham cracker squares

½ cup packed brown sugar

½ cup butter

½ teaspoon vanilla

½ cup chopped pecans

1 Heat oven to 350°F. Arrange graham crackers in single layer in ungreased 15x10x1-inch jelly roll pan.

2 In 2-quart saucepan, heat brown sugar and butter to boiling. Boil 1 minute, stirring constantly. Remove from heat; stir in vanilla. Pour mixture over graham crackers; spread evenly. Sprinkle with pecans.

3 Bake 8 to 10 minutes or until bubbly. Cool 5 minutes. Cut between graham crackers into bars.

1 Bar: Calories 95; Total Fat 6g (Saturated Fat 1g, Trans Fat 0g); Cholesterol 0mg; Sodium 85mg; Total Carbohydrate 10g (Dietary Fiber 0g); Protein 0g **Exchanges:** ½ Starch, 1 Fat **Carbohydrate Choices:** ½

The Wow Factor If any bars break while cutting them, fold them into softened vanilla ice cream for a delicious twist. Serve immediately.

Salty Caramel-Peanut Brittle Bars

48 bars | Prep Time: 15 Minutes | Start to Finish: 2 Hours 5 Minutes

1 pouch (1 lb 1.5 oz) sugar cookie mix

¼ cup packed brown sugar

¾ cup cold butter

2 cups salted cocktail peanuts

1 cup semisweet chocolate chips

1 jar (12.25 oz) caramel topping

½ teaspoon coarse sea salt

1 Heat oven to 350°F. Spray bottom and sides of 15x10x1-inch jelly roll pan with cooking spray. Reserve 3 tablespoons cookie mix for topping.

2 Place remaining cookie mix in large bowl. Stir in brown sugar. Cut in butter, using pastry blender or fork, until mixture looks like coarse crumbs. Press mixture in bottom of pan. Bake 18 minutes.

3 Immediately sprinkle peanuts and chocolate chips over hot crust. In small microwavable bowl, microwave caramel topping uncovered on High about 30 seconds or until drizzling consistency. Add reserved cookie mix; blend well. Drizzle over peanuts and chocolate chips. Sprinkle with salt.

4 Bake 12 to 14 minutes or until caramel is bubbly. Cool completely in pan on cooling rack, about 1 hour.

5 Refrigerate 15 minutes to set chocolate. Cut into 8 rows by 6 rows. Store covered at room temperature.

1 Bar: Calories 150; Total Fat 8g (Saturated Fat 3g, Trans Fat 0g); Cholesterol 10mg; Sodium 130mg; Total Carbohydrate 17g (Dietary Fiber 0g); Protein 2g
Exchanges: ½ Starch, ½ Other Carbohydrate, 1½ Fat **Carbohydrate Choices:** 1

The Wow Factor Wrap up some of these bars in a gift box for a perfect hostess gift or thank-you.

Neapolitan Cream Cheese Bars

36 bars | Prep Time: 15 Minutes | Start to Finish: 3 Hours 40 Minutes

1 pouch (1 lb 1.5 oz) double chocolate chunk cookie mix

½ cup butter, melted

3 eggs

2 packages (8 oz each) cream cheese, softened

½ cup sugar

1 teaspoon vanilla

1 container (12 oz) strawberry whipped ready-to-spread frosting

1 Heat oven to 350°F. Spray bottom and sides of 13x9-inch pan with cooking spray.

2 In large bowl, stir cookie mix, melted butter and 1 of the eggs until soft dough forms. Press dough in bottom of pan. Bake 10 minutes. Cool 10 minutes.

3 In large bowl, beat cream cheese, sugar, vanilla and remaining 2 eggs with electric mixer on medium speed until smooth. Spread over cookie base.

4 Bake 30 to 35 minutes or until set. Cool in pan on cooling rack 30 minutes.

5 Spread frosting over cream cheese layer. Refrigerate about 2 hours or until chilled. Cut into 6 rows by 6 rows. Store covered in refrigerator.

1 Bar: Calories 180; Total Fat 11g (Saturated Fat 6g, Trans Fat 1g); Cholesterol 40mg; Sodium 135mg; Total Carbohydrate 20g (Dietary Fiber 0g); Protein 1g **Exchanges:** ½ Starch, 1 Other Carbohydrate, 2 Fat **Carbohydrate Choices:** 1

Sweet Success Use a wet knife for cutting cheesecake bars, wiping off crumbs after each cut.

Heavenly Chocolate Mousse Bars

36 bars | Prep Time: 20 Minutes | Start to Finish: 2 Hours 5 Minutes

1   pouch (1 lb 1.5 oz) sugar cookie mix

½   cup butter, melted

1   egg

2   cups semisweet chocolate chips (about 12 oz)

1   package (8 oz) cream cheese, softened

1½   cups whipping cream

1   Heat oven to 350°F. In medium bowl, stir cookie mix, butter and egg until soft dough forms. Spread dough in bottom of ungreased 13x9-inch pan. Bake 12 to 15 minutes or until light golden brown. Cool completely in pan on cooling rack.

2   In small microwavable bowl, microwave 1 cup of the chocolate chips uncovered on High 1 to 2 minutes, stirring once, until softened and chips can be stirred smooth. In medium bowl, beat cream cheese with electric mixer on medium speed until smooth. Add melted chocolate; stir until blended.

3   In small bowl, beat 1 cup of the whipping cream with electric mixer on high speed until stiff peaks form. Fold whipped cream into chocolate–cream cheese mixture until well blended. Spread over cooled cookie base. Cover; refrigerate 1 hour or until set.

4   In small microwavable bowl, microwave remaining 1 cup chocolate chips uncovered on High 1 to 2 minutes, stirring once, until softened and chips can be stirred smooth. Stir in remaining ½ cup whipping cream until blended. Spoon warm chocolate mixture over mousse layer; spread evenly.

5   Refrigerate 30 minutes or until set. Cut into 9 rows by 4 rows. Store tightly covered in refrigerator.

1 Bar: Calories 180; Total Fat 12g (Saturated Fat 7g, Trans Fat 0g); Cholesterol 0mg; Sodium 85mg; Total Carbohydrate 17g (Dietary Fiber 0g); Protein 1g
Exchanges: 1 Other Carbohydrate, 2½ Fat **Carbohydrate Choices:** 1

Other Than Square

All bars dream of the day when they can have a new shape—now is their chance! Break out of the ho-hum square and rectangle doldrums by cutting your bars in some fresh, exciting ways.

TRIANGULATION Simply cut squares diagonally in half, creating two triangles. Double the eating pleasure—without any guilt!

BARS WITH AN EDGE Instead of cutting perfectly perpendicular rows, start by cutting the first row slightly askew. Cut rows parallel to this one. Repeat on the other side, creating "edgy" bars.

Or create diamonds by making your first cut in a pan of bars, diagonally from one corner to the other, and then cutting rows parallel to this one. Repeat on the other side, cutting between the other, opposite corners and making cuts parallel to it. (There will be some small edge pieces that aren't large enough to serve. Use these to taste test your creation or to offer to guests who can't wait to try your bars.)

PICK-UP STICKS Cut bars into sticks instead of bars (for a 13x9-inch pan, try cutting 8 rows by 6 rows). If you wish, sturdy bars can be dipped into melted chocolate and placed on waxed paper or parchment to dry. (See Brownie Pops, page 202, adjusting the amount of chocolate and shortening as needed for bar sticks.)

TAKE ON SHAPE Use cookie cutters to cut bars into unique shapes. Cutters with simple lines and large, open areas will work the best (so pieces of the bar don't get stuck in small spaces of intricate shapes). Bars without a lot of nuts or chocolate chips or sticky layers will be the easiest to cut with cutters. Spray inside of cutter with cooking spray if the bars stick to it, and release the bars from cutter onto serving plate by gently pressing on bar with back of spoon.

FESTIVE TREES Cut bars into triangles. Insert candy stick into base end to resemble Christmas tree. Decorate trees with frosting and sprinkles as desired.

How Many?

Wondering, if you cut your bars a certain way, how many you will have? Here's a handy chart to refer to when making sheet pans of bars. (For shapes other than squares or rectangles, the yield will be different depending on the sizes cut with scraps leftover.)

PAN	NUMBER OF ROWS	APPROXIMATE SIZE (in inches)	YIELD
13 x 9	8 x 4	1⅝ x 2¼	32
	6 x 6	2⅛ x 1½	36
	8 x 5	1⅝ x 1¾	40
	8 x 6	1⅝ x 1½	48
	6 x 9	2⅛ x 1	54
15 x 10 x 1	10 x 4	1½ x 2⅝	40
	8 x 6	1⅞ x 1¾	48
	10 x 5	1½ x 2	50
	9 x 6	1¾ x 1¾	54
	10 x 6	1½ x 1¾	60

Pecan-Praline Bacon Bars

32 bars | Prep Time: 20 Minutes | Start to Finish: 2 Hours

CRUST

1½	cups all-purpose flour
½	cup packed dark brown sugar
1	cup butter, softened
1	package (2.1 oz) precooked bacon, cut into ¼-inch slices

FROSTING

½	cup whipping cream
⅓	cup butter
1½	cups packed dark brown sugar
1½	cups powdered sugar
1	teaspoon vanilla
1½	cups pecan halves

1 Heat oven to 325°F. In medium bowl, stir together flour and ½ cup brown sugar. Beat in 1 cup butter with electric mixer on medium speed until blended; stir in bacon. Press in bottom of ungreased 13x9-inch pan.

2 Bake 20 to 25 minutes or until center is set. Cool completely in pan on cooling rack, about 30 minutes.

3 In 1-quart saucepan, heat whipping cream, ⅓ cup butter and 1½ cups brown sugar to boiling over medium heat, stirring frequently. Boil and stir 1 minute; remove from heat. Stir in powdered sugar and the vanilla with whisk until smooth. Spread frosting over cooled baked crust. Arrange pecans over frosting.

4 Let stand 30 to 45 minutes until frosting is set but not firm. Cut into 8 rows by 4 rows. Store covered in refrigerator.

1 Bar: Calories 220; Total Fat 13g (Saturated Fat 6g, Trans Fat 0g); Cholesterol 25mg; Sodium 105mg; Total Carbohydrate 24g (Dietary Fiber 0g); Protein 2g **Exchanges:** ½ Starch, 1 Other Carbohydrate, 2½ Fat **Carbohydrate Choices:** 1½

Sweet Success To prevent frosting from cracking, be sure to cut bars 30 to 45 minutes after frosting. Frosting will be slightly warm but set.

Triple-Nut Bars

36 bars | Prep Time: 35 Minutes | Start to Finish: 2 Hours 10 Minutes

CRUST

- ¾ cup butter, softened
- ½ cup packed brown sugar
- ½ teaspoon almond extract
- 1½ cups all-purpose flour

TOPPING

- 1 cup butter, cut into pieces
- 1½ cups packed brown sugar
- ¼ cup honey
- ¼ cup light corn syrup
- ½ teaspoon vanilla
- 1 cup walnut pieces
- 1 cup unblanched or blanched whole almonds
- 1 cup pecan halves

1 Heat oven to 350°F. In medium bowl, beat ¾ cup butter, ½ cup brown sugar and the almond extract with electric mixer on medium-low speed until blended. On low speed, beat in flour until soft dough forms. Press dough in bottom of ungreased 13x9-inch pan. Bake 17 to 20 minutes or until golden brown.

2 Meanwhile, in 2-quart saucepan, cook 1 cup butter, 1½ cups brown sugar, the honey and corn syrup over medium-high heat 12 to 15 minutes, stirring frequently, until mixture comes to a full rolling boil. Boil 1 to 2 minutes, stirring frequently. Remove from heat. Stir in vanilla.

3 Sprinkle walnuts, almonds and pecans over partially baked crust. Pour brown sugar mixture over nuts.

4 Bake 13 to 15 minutes or until top is bubbly. Cool completely in pan on cooling rack, about 1 hour. Cut into 6 rows by 6 rows.

1 Bar: Calories 230; Total Fat 15g (Saturated Fat 6g, Trans Fat 0g); Cholesterol 25mg; Sodium 70mg; Total Carbohydrate 21g (Dietary Fiber 1g); Protein 2g
Exchanges: 1½ Other Carbohydrate, 3 Fat **Carbohydrate Choices:** 1½

The Wow Factor For an extra layer of indulgence, drizzle the bars with about ⅓ cup of caramel topping. Sprinkle lightly with coarse sea salt.

Pecan Pie Bars

36 bars | Prep Time: 15 Minutes | Start to Finish: 2 Hours 5 Minutes

⅔ cup granulated sugar

½ cup butter, softened

2 teaspoons vanilla extract

1½ cups all-purpose flour

⅔ cup packed brown sugar

½ cup light or dark corn syrup

¼ teaspoon salt

3 eggs

1 cup coarsely chopped pecans

1 Heat oven to 350°F. Lightly grease bottom and sides of 13x9-inch pan with shortening or cooking spray.

2 In large bowl, mix granulated sugar, butter and 1 teaspoon of the vanilla. Stir in flour. Press dough in bottom and ½ inch up sides of pan. Bake 15 to 17 minutes or until edges are light brown.

3 In medium bowl, beat brown sugar, corn syrup, salt, eggs and remaining 1 teaspoon vanilla with spoon. Stir in pecans. Pour over partially baked crust.

4 Bake 25 to 30 minutes or until set. Run knife around sides of pan to loosen edges. Cool completely in pan on cooling rack, about 1 hour. Cut into 9 rows by 4 rows.

1 Bar: Calories 120; Total Fat 5g (Saturated Fat 2g, Trans Fat 0g); Cholesterol 20mg; Sodium 45mg; Total Carbohydrate 16g (Dietary Fiber 0g); Protein 1g **Exchanges:** ½ Starch, ½ Other Carbohydrate, 1 Fat **Carbohydrate Choices:** 1

The Wow Factor Cut the bars diagonally in half, then dip one end of each bar in melted chocolate; lay flat on waxed paper until chocolate is set. Use your favorite chocolate chips—milk, semisweet or dark—or chopped chocolate baking bars or candy bars.

Caramel Peanut-Popcorn Squares

24 bars | Prep Time: 20 Minutes | Start to Finish: 2 Hours 15 Minutes

1 roll (16.5 oz) refrigerated peanut butter cookies

3½ cups miniature marshmallows

1 bag (3 oz) butter-flavored microwave popcorn, popped (8 cups)

1 cup lightly salted dry-roasted peanuts

1⅔ cups peanut butter chips

⅔ cup light corn syrup

¼ cup butter

1 cup semisweet chocolate chips

1 Heat oven to 350°F. Spray bottom and sides of 13x9-inch pan with cooking spray. With floured fingers, press cookie dough in bottom of pan to form crust.

2 Bake 14 to 16 minutes or until light golden brown. Sprinkle marshmallows over crust. Bake 3 minutes longer or until marshmallows are puffed but not browned.

3 Meanwhile, remove and discard unpopped kernels from popped popcorn. In large bowl, mix popcorn and peanuts; set aside.

4 In medium microwavable bowl, microwave peanut butter chips, corn syrup and butter uncovered on High 1 to 2 minutes, stirring every 30 seconds, until melted and smooth. Pour over popcorn mixture; stir to coat completely. Immediately press mixture over marshmallows in even layer, using back of spoon.

5 In small microwavable bowl, microwave chocolate chips uncovered on High 1 minute to 1 minute 30 seconds, stirring every 30 seconds, until softened and chips can be stirred smooth. Drizzle melted chocolate over bars. Cool completely in pan on cooling rack, about 1 hour. Refrigerate 30 minutes or until set. Cut into 6 rows by 4 rows.

1 Bar: Calories 330; Total Fat 16g (Saturated Fat 9g, Trans Fat 0g); Cholesterol 0mg; Sodium 180mg; Total Carbohydrate 39g (Dietary Fiber 1.5g); Protein 7g **Exchanges:** ½ Starch, 1½ Other Carbohydrate, 1 High-Fat Meat, 2 Fat **Carbohydrate Choices:** 2

The Wow Factor Substitute 8 cups of popped caramel corn with nuts or even cheese popcorn for the butter-flavored popcorn for an extra-special twist on these bars.

Elegant Almond Bars

32 bars | Prep Time: 25 Minutes | Start to Finish: 2 Hours 35 Minutes

COOKIE BASE

- 1 pouch (1 lb 1.5 oz) sugar cookie mix
- ½ cup butter, melted
- ½ teaspoon almond extract
- 1 egg

FILLING

- 1 can (8 oz) or 1 package (7 oz) almond paste, crumbled into ½-inch pieces
- ¼ cup sugar
- ¼ cup butter, melted
- 2 eggs
- ½ cup sliced almonds

TOPPING

- 2 oz white chocolate baking bar, coarsely chopped (⅓ cup)
- 2 tablespoons shortening
- ¼ cup sliced almonds

1 Heat oven to 350°F. In large bowl, stir cookie base ingredients until soft dough forms. Spread dough in ungreased 13x9-inch pan. Bake 15 to 18 minutes or until light golden brown.

2 Meanwhile, in large bowl, beat almond paste, sugar and ¼ cup butter with electric mixer on low speed until blended. Add 2 eggs; beat until well blended (mixture may be slightly lumpy).

3 Spread almond paste mixture over partially baked base. Sprinkle with ½ cup almonds. Bake 15 to 20 minutes or until filling is set (filling will puff up during baking). Cool completely in pan on cooling rack, about 1 hour.

4 In 1-quart saucepan, melt white chocolate and shortening over low heat, stirring constantly, until smooth. Pour and spread over cooled bars. Sprinkle with ¼ cup almonds. Let stand about 30 minutes or until topping is set. Cut into 8 rows by 4 rows. Store covered at room temperature.

1 Bar: Calories 180; Total Fat 10g (Saturated Fat 4g, Trans Fat 1g); Cholesterol 30mg; Sodium 75mg; Total Carbohydrate 19g (Dietary Fiber 0g); Protein 3g **Exchanges:** 1½ Other Carbohydrate, ½ High-Fat Meat, 1 Fat **Carbohydrate Choices:** 1

The Wow Factor For a large gathering, make up a tray of 3 different types of bars. Vary the colors, textures and flavors of the bars for a nice variety. An irresistible combination would be Apple Streusel Cheesecake Bars (page 168) and Chocolate Truffle–Topped Caramel Bars (page 118) with these almond bars. Also vary the shapes of the bars. See Other Than Square (page 146).

Holiday Peppermint-Marshmallow Bites

24 bars | Prep Time: 10 Minutes | Start to Finish: 1 Hour 10 Minutes

1 bag (10.5 oz) miniature marshmallows (5½ cups)

¼ cup butter

2 bags (10.5 oz each) Chex Mix™ Muddy Buddies™ Peppermint Bark snack mix

1 Butter bottom and sides of 13x9-inch pan. In large microwavable bowl, microwave marshmallows and ¼ cup butter uncovered on High about 2 minutes, stirring after every minute, until melted and smooth. Immediately stir in snack mix. Press mixture in pan.

2 Let stand at room temperature about 1 hour or until firm. Cut into 6 rows by 4 rows. Store tightly covered at room temperature up to 2 days.

1 Bar: Calories 170; Total Fat 5g (Saturated Fat 4g, Trans Fat 0g); Cholesterol 5mg; Sodium 55mg; Total Carbohydrate 29g (Dietary Fiber 0g); Protein 1g **Exchanges:** ½ Starch, 1½ Other Carbohydrate, 1 Fat **Carbohydrate Choices:** 2

Sweet Success Chex Mix Muddy Buddies Peppermint Bark snack mix is only available during the holidays, but you can make this recipe any time of the year by substituting Muddy Buddies™ Brownie Supreme snack mix instead.

Gluten-Free Peanut Butter and Jam Cookie Bars

24 bars | Prep Time: 25 Minutes | Start to Finish: 2 Hours 25 Minutes

1¼	cups gluten-free old-fashioned oats
½	cup white rice flour
½	cup almond flour
¼	cup gluten-free oat flour
¼	cup tapioca flour
1	teaspoon gluten-free baking powder
½	teaspoon baking soda
1	cup coarsely chopped salted peanuts
½	cup butter, softened
½	cup sugar
½	cup creamy peanut butter
2	eggs
1	jar (12 oz) gluten-free grape jam

1 Heat oven to 350°F. Spray bottom and sides of 13x9-inch pan with cooking spray (without flour).

2 In medium bowl, mix oats, flours, baking powder, baking soda and ¾ cup of the peanuts with whisk; set aside. In large bowl, beat butter, sugar and peanut butter with electric mixer on medium speed until blended. Beat in eggs. Gradually add oat mixture, beating on low speed just until combined.

3 Press two-thirds (about 3½ cups) of the dough in pan. Spread jam over crust. Drop heaping spoonfuls of remaining dough over jam. Sprinkle with remaining ¼ cup peanuts.

4 Bake 25 to 30 minutes or until set and golden brown. Cool completely in pan on cooling rack, about 1 hour. Refrigerate 30 minutes. Cut into 6 rows by 4 rows. Store in refrigerator.

1 Bar: Calories 220; Total Fat 12g (Saturated Fat 3.5g, Trans Fat 0g); Cholesterol 30mg; Sodium 130mg; Total Carbohydrate 24g (Dietary Fiber 2g); Protein 5g **Exchanges:** 1 Starch, ½ Other Carbohydrate, 2½ Fat **Carbohydrate Choices:** 1½

Sweet Success Substitute almond butter for the peanut butter and salted almonds for the peanuts, if you like, and use your family's favorite jam in place of the grape jam.

Cooking Gluten Free? Always read labels to make sure each recipe ingredient is gluten free. Products and ingredient sources can change.

Baklava Bars

24 bars | Prep Time: 25 Minutes | Start to Finish: 3 Hours

COOKIE BASE

- 1 pouch (1 lb 1.5 oz) sugar cookie mix
- ½ cup butter, softened
- ½ teaspoon grated lemon peel
- 1 egg

FILLING

- 1½ cups chopped walnuts
- ⅓ cup granulated sugar
- ¼ cup butter, softened
- 1 teaspoon cinnamon
- ⅛ teaspoon salt
- 8 frozen mini fillo shells (from 1.9-oz package)

GLAZE

- ⅓ cup honey
- 2 tablespoons butter, softened
- 1 tablespoon packed brown sugar
- ½ teaspoon lemon juice
- ¼ teaspoon ground cinnamon
- 1 teaspoon vanilla

GARNISH

- 5 tablespoons honey

1 Heat oven to 350°F. Spray bottom only of 13x9-inch pan with cooking spray.

2 In large bowl, stir cookie base ingredients until soft dough forms. Press dough in bottom of pan. Bake 15 minutes.

3 Meanwhile, in medium bowl, stir walnuts, granulated sugar, ¼ cup butter, 1 teaspoon cinnamon and the salt with fork until mixture is well blended and crumbly.

4 Sprinkle nut mixture over partially baked base. With hands, crumble frozen fillo shells over nut mixture. Bake 18 to 20 minutes or until golden brown.

5 In small microwavable bowl, microwave ⅓ cup honey, 2 tablespoons butter, the brown sugar, lemon juice and ¼ teaspoon cinnamon uncovered on High 1 minute or until bubbly. Stir in vanilla. Drizzle glaze over fillo. Cool completely in pan on cooling rack, about 2 hours.

6 Cut into 4 rows by 3 rows, then cut each bar diagonally in half. Before serving, drizzle about ½ teaspoon honey over each bar. Store covered at room temperature.

1 Bar: Calories 250; Total Fat 14g (Saturated Fat 5g, Trans Fat 1g); Cholesterol 25mg; Sodium 115mg; Total Carbohydrate 29g (Dietary Fiber 0g); Protein 2g **Exchanges:** ½ Starch, 1½ Other Carbohydrate, 2½ Fat **Carbohydrate Choices:** 2

Crème Brûlée Cheesecake Bars

36 bars | Prep Time: 20 Minutes | Start to Finish: 4 Hours 25 Minutes

1   pouch (1 lb 1.5 oz) sugar cookie mix

1   box (4-serving size) French vanilla instant pudding and pie filling mix

2   tablespoons packed brown sugar

½   cup butter, melted

2½   teaspoons vanilla

2   whole eggs

2   packages (8 oz each) cream cheese, softened

½   cup sour cream

½   cup granulated sugar

3   egg yolks

⅔   cup toffee bits, finely crushed

1 Heat oven to 350°F. Lightly spray bottom and sides of 13x9-inch pan with cooking spray.

2 In large bowl, stir cookie mix, dry pudding mix, brown sugar, butter, 1 teaspoon of the vanilla and 1 whole egg until soft dough forms. Press dough in bottom and ½ inch up sides of pan.

3 In medium bowl, beat cream cheese, sour cream and granulated sugar with electric mixer on medium speed until smooth. Add remaining whole egg, 3 egg yolks and remaining 1½ teaspoons vanilla; beat until smooth. Spread over crust in pan.

4 Bake 30 to 35 minutes or until set in center. Immediately sprinkle crushed toffee bits over top. Cool in pan on cooling rack 30 minutes.

5 Refrigerate about 3 hours or until chilled. Cut into 9 rows by 4 rows. Store covered in refrigerator.

1 Bar: Calories 190; Total Fat 11g (Saturated Fat 6g, Trans Fat 1g); Cholesterol 55mg; Sodium 160mg; Total Carbohydrate 20g (Dietary Fiber 0g); Protein 2g **Exchanges:** ½ Starch, 1 Other Carbohydrate, 2 Fat **Carbohydrate Choices:** 1

Sweet Success To crush the toffee bits, place in a small resealable food-storage plastic bag; pound with a rolling pin or flat side of a meat mallet.

Eggnog Cheesecake Bars

24 bars | Prep Time: 25 Minutes | Start to Finish: 2 Hours 40 Minutes

CRUST

- 2 cups graham cracker crumbs (about 30 squares)
- ¾ cup butter, melted
- ½ cup blanched whole almonds, finely chopped
- ¼ cup packed brown sugar
- 1 tablespoon ground cinnamon

FILLING

- 2 packages (8 oz each) cream cheese, softened
- ¼ cup granulated sugar
- ¼ cup packed brown sugar
- 2 teaspoons ground nutmeg
- ½ cup whipping cream
- 1 teaspoon vanilla
- 2 eggs

TOPPING

- ½ cup blanched whole almonds, finely chopped, toasted*

1 Heat oven to 350°F. In large bowl, stir crust ingredients until well blended. Press mixture in bottom of ungreased 13x9-inch pan. Bake 8 minutes.

2 In another large bowl, beat cream cheese with electric mixer on medium speed until softened. Gradually beat in granulated sugar, ¼ cup brown sugar, the nutmeg, whipping cream and vanilla. Beat in eggs, one at a time, until creamy. Pour filling over crust.

3 Bake 30 to 35 minutes or until center is set. Sprinkle with toasted almonds; press in slightly. Cool in pan on cooling rack 1 hour 30 minutes.

4 Cut into 6 rows by 4 rows, using thin knife and wiping blade occasionally. Store covered in refrigerator.

*To toast chopped almonds, bake in ungreased shallow pan at 350°F 3 to 5 minutes, stirring occasionally, until golden brown.

1 Bar: Calories 460; Total Fat 36g (Saturated Fat 19g, Trans Fat 1g); Cholesterol 110mg; Sodium 300mg; Total Carbohydrate 28g (Dietary Fiber 2g); Protein 7g **Exchanges:** 2 Other Carbohydrate, 1 High-Fat Meat, 5½ Fat **Carbohydrate Choices:** 2

Sweet Success Try crushed vanilla wafer cookies instead of the graham cracker crumbs.

Apple Streusel Cheesecake Bars

24 bars | Prep Time: 20 Minutes | Start to Finish: 3 Hours 40 Minutes

1   pouch (1 lb 1.5 oz) oatmeal cookie mix

½   cup cold butter

2   packages (8 oz each) cream cheese, softened

½   cup sugar

2   tablespoons all-purpose flour

1   teaspoon vanilla

1   egg

1   can (21 oz) apple pie filling

½   teaspoon ground cinnamon

¼   cup chopped walnuts

1 Heat oven to 350°F. Spray bottom only of 13x9-inch pan with cooking spray.

2 In large bowl, place cookie mix. Cut in butter, using pastry blender or fork, until mixture looks like coarse crumbs. Reserve 1½ cups crumb mixture; press remaining crumbs in bottom of pan. Bake 10 minutes.

3 In medium bowl, beat cream cheese, sugar, flour, vanilla and egg with electric mixer on medium speed until smooth. Spread cream cheese mixture over partially baked crust.

4 In medium bowl, mix pie filling and cinnamon. Spoon over cream cheese mixture. Sprinkle reserved crumbs over top. Sprinkle with walnuts.

5 Bake 35 to 40 minutes or until light golden brown. Cool in pan on cooling rack 30 minutes. Refrigerate until chilled, about 2 hours. Cut into 6 rows by 4 rows. Store covered in refrigerator.

1 Bar: Calories 240; Total Fat 12g (Saturated Fat 7g, Trans Fat 0g); Cholesterol 40mg; Sodium 160mg; Total Carbohydrate 29g (Dietary Fiber 0g); Protein 3g **Exchanges:** 1 Starch, 1 Other Carbohydrate, 2 Fat **Carbohydrate Choices:** 2

Apple Crumble Bars

24 bars | Prep Time: 15 Minutes | Start to Finish: 3 Hours 40 Minutes

CRUST

2½	cups all-purpose flour
1	cup butter or margarine, softened
¾	cup granulated sugar
½	teaspoon salt

FILLING

3½	cups apple pie filling (from two 21-oz cans)

CRUMBLE

1	cup all-purpose flour
1	cup quick-cooking oats
¾	cup packed brown sugar
1	teaspoon ground cinnamon
¼	teaspoon ground nutmeg
10	tablespoons butter, cut into small pieces

1 Heat oven to 375°F. Grease 13x9-inch pan with shortening or cooking spray. In large bowl, beat crust ingredients with electric mixer on low speed until mixture looks like coarse crumbs. Press in pan.

2 Bake 15 minutes or until golden brown. Cool about 30 minutes. Reduce oven temperature to 350°F.

3 Spoon pie filling evenly over crust. In medium bowl, mix 1 cup flour, the oats, brown sugar, cinnamon and nutmeg. Add 10 tablespoons butter; mix with fork or fingers until crumbly. Sprinkle mixture evenly over filling; press lightly.

4 Bake 40 minutes or until light brown. Cool completely in pan on cooling rack, about 2 hours. Cut into 6 rows by 4 rows.

1 Serving: Calories 283; Total Fat 13g (Saturated Fat 8g, Trans Fat 0.5g); Cholesterol 35mg; Sodium 75mg; Total Carbohydrate 41g (Dietary Fiber 1g); Protein 3g **Exchanges:** 1 Starch, 1½ Other Carbohydrate, 2½ Fat **Carbohydrate Choices:** 2½

The Wow Factor Serve these delicious bars up, pie style. Top each with a scoop of cinnamon or vanilla ice cream and a drizzle of caramel sauce—yum!

Banana-Cashew Bars

24 bars | Prep Time: 30 Minutes | Start to Finish: 1 Hour 40 Minutes

BARS

1	cup granulated sugar
1	cup mashed very ripe bananas (2 medium)
⅓	cup butter, softened
2	eggs
1	cup all-purpose flour
1	teaspoon baking powder
½	teaspoon baking soda
¼	teaspoon salt
½	cup chopped cashews

FROSTING

½	cup butter*
3¼	cups powdered sugar
1	teaspoon vanilla
1	to 3 tablespoons milk

GARNISH

24	cashew halves, if desired

1 Heat oven to 350°F. Grease bottom and sides of 13x9-inch pan with shortening or cooking spray.

2 In large bowl, mix granulated sugar, bananas, ⅓ cup butter and the eggs until blended. Stir in flour, baking powder, baking soda and salt until combined. Stir in chopped cashews. Spread batter in pan.

3 Bake 22 to 26 minutes or until toothpick inserted in center comes out clean. Cool completely in pan on cooling rack, about 40 minutes.

4 In 2-quart saucepan, heat ½ cup butter over medium heat, stirring constantly, until golden brown. (Watch carefully to make sure it doesn't burn.) Remove from heat. Using spoon, gradually beat in powdered sugar. Stir in vanilla and the milk, 1 tablespoon at a time, until frosting is smooth and desired consistency. Immediately frost bars.

5 Score bars into 6 rows by 4 rows, making shallow cuts in frosting. Top center of each bar with cashew half, pressing in lightly. Cut bars on scored lines.

*Do not use margarine or vegetable oil spreads in the frosting.

1 Bar: Calories 210; Total Fat 8g (Saturated Fat 4.5g, Trans Fat 0g); Cholesterol 35mg; Sodium 125mg; Total Carbohydrate 32g (Dietary Fiber 0g); Protein 1g
Exchanges: ½ Starch, 1½ Other Carbohydrate, 1½ Fat **Carbohydrate Choices:** 2

Sweet Success Since the browned butter frosting sets up quickly, do not make it until the bars have cooled.

Easy Berry Bars

48 bars | Prep Time: 10 Minutes | Start to Finish: 1 Hour 35 Minutes

1 box (15.25 oz) yellow cake mix with pudding in the mix

1 cup butter, softened

2 eggs

1 container (12 oz) fluffy white whipped ready-to-spread frosting

4 cups fresh berries (raspberries, blueberries, sliced strawberries)

Fresh mint leaves, if desired

1 Heat oven to 350°F (325°F for dark or nonstick pan). Spray bottom and sides of 15x10x1-inch jelly roll pan with baking spray with flour.

2 In large bowl, beat cake mix, butter and eggs with electric mixer on medium speed about 2 minutes or until well blended. Spread batter in pan.

3 Bake 19 to 24 minutes or until top is golden brown and toothpick inserted in center comes out clean. Cool completely in pan on cooling rack, about 1 hour.

4 Spread frosting over bars. Cut into 8 rows by 6 rows. Top with berries up to 2 hours before serving. Garnish with mint. Store covered in refrigerator.

1 Bar: Calories 110; Total Fat 6g (Saturated Fat 3g, Trans Fat 0.5g); Cholesterol 20mg; Sodium 110mg; Total Carbohydrate 13g (Dietary Fiber 0g); Protein 0g **Exchanges:** 1 Other Carbohydrate, 1 Fat **Carbohydrate Choices:** 1

Sweet Success Be sure your berries are dry before topping the bars, so the colors won't bleed onto the frosting. Place them on paper towels while the bars cool.

Fresh Berry Dessert Bites

40 bars | Prep Time: 30 Minutes | Start to Finish: 2 Hours 30 Minutes

CRUST

2¼	cups all-purpose flour
⅔	cup granulated sugar
½	teaspoon grated lemon peel
¼	teaspoon salt
1	cup cold butter

TOPPING

1	package (8 oz) cream cheese, softened
2	tablespoons packed brown sugar
1	container (6 oz) lemon fat-free yogurt
1	teaspoon grated lemon peel
40	fresh raspberries (about 6 oz)
40	fresh blackberries (about 8 oz)
40	fresh blueberries (about 3 oz)

1 Heat oven to 350°F. Grease bottom and sides of 15x10x1-inch jelly roll pan with shortening or cooking spray.

2 In large bowl, mix flour, granulated sugar, ½ teaspoon lemon peel and the salt. Cut in butter, using pastry blender or fork, until mixture looks like fine crumbs. Press mixture in bottom of pan.

3 Bake 18 to 20 minutes or until edges are light golden. Cool completely in pan on cooling rack, about 40 minutes.

4 In medium bowl, beat cream cheese and brown sugar with electric mixer on low speed until blended. Add yogurt and 1 teaspoon lemon peel; beat until blended. Spread mixture over crust. Refrigerate at least 1 hour but no longer than 24 hours.

5 Cut into 10 rows by 4 rows. Arrange 1 of each kind of berry on each bar. Store in refrigerator.

1 Bar: Calories 110; Total Fat 7g (Saturated Fat 4g, Trans Fat 0g); Cholesterol 20mg; Sodium 65mg; Total Carbohydrate 12g (Dietary Fiber 0g); Protein 1g **Exchanges:** ½ Starch, 1½ Fat **Carbohydrate Choices:** 1

Sweet Success Vanilla, raspberry or strawberry yogurt can be substituted for the lemon.

Blueberry Cheesecake Bars

28 bars | Prep Time: 20 Minutes | Start to Finish: 4 Hours

1   pouch (1 lb 1.5 oz) oatmeal cookie mix

½   cup butter, softened

1   egg

3   packages (8 oz each) cream cheese, softened

¾   cup sugar

½   cup whipping cream

3   eggs

1   jar (10 oz) blueberry spreadable fruit

1½   cups fresh or frozen (thawed and drained) blueberries

1 Heat oven to 350°F. Spray bottom and sides of 13x9-inch pan with cooking spray.

2 In medium bowl, beat cookie mix, butter and egg with electric mixer on low speed until soft dough forms. Press dough in bottom of pan. Bake 15 minutes. Cool 10 minutes.

3 Meanwhile, in large bowl, beat cream cheese and sugar with electric mixer on medium speed until fluffy. Add whipping cream and eggs; beat on low speed until well blended.

4 Spread spreadable fruit over partially baked crust; sprinkle with blueberries. Spoon cream cheese mixture evenly over blueberries, spreading gently to cover.

5 Bake 40 to 45 minutes or until center is set. Cool in pan on cooling rack 30 minutes. Refrigerate at least 2 hours. Cut into 7 rows by 4 rows. Store covered in refrigerator.

1 Bar: Calories 260; Total Fat 14g (Saturated Fat 8g, Trans Fat 0g); Cholesterol 70mg; Sodium 180mg; Total Carbohydrate 28g (Dietary Fiber 1g); Protein 4g **Exchanges:** ½ Starch, 1½ Other Carbohydrate, 3 Fat **Carbohydrate Choices:** 2

Cherry Cheesecake Bars

24 bars | Prep Time: 30 Minutes | Start to Finish: 3 Hours 55 Minutes

COOKIE BASE

- 1 pouch (1 lb 1.5 oz) sugar cookie mix
- ¼ cup cold butter
- 4 oz (half of 8-oz package) cream cheese

FILLING

- 20 oz (two and a half 8-oz packages) cream cheese, softened
- ½ cup sugar
- 2 tablespoons all-purpose flour
- 1 teaspoon almond extract
- 2 eggs
- 1 can (21 oz) cherry pie filling

TOPPING

- 1½ cups reserved cookie base mixture
- ½ cup sliced almonds

1 Heat oven to 350°F. Spray bottom and sides of 13x9-inch pan with cooking spray.

2 Place cookie mix in large bowl. Cut in butter and 4 oz cream cheese, using pastry blender or fork, until mixture is crumbly. Reserve 1½ cups mixture for topping. Press remaining mixture in bottom of pan. Bake 12 minutes.

3 Meanwhile, in large bowl, beat 20 oz cream cheese, the sugar, flour, almond extract and eggs with electric mixer on medium speed until smooth.

4 Spread cream cheese mixture over partially baked cookie base. Spoon pie filling over cream cheese layer. Sprinkle with reserved cookie base mixture and the almonds.

5 Bake 40 to 45 minutes or until light golden brown. Cool in pan on cooling rack 30 minutes. Refrigerate about 2 hours or until chilled. Cut into 6 rows by 4 rows. Store covered in refrigerator.

1 Bar: Calories 270; Total Fat 15g (Saturated Fat 8g, Trans Fat 1g); Cholesterol 55mg; Sodium 160mg; Total Carbohydrate 28g (Dietary Fiber 0g); Protein 4g **Exchanges:** 1 Starch, 1 Other Carbohydrate, 3 Fat **Carbohydrate Choices:** 2

Cranberry Crumb Bars

24 bars | Prep Time: 20 Minutes | Start to Finish: 4 Hours 15 Minutes

CRUST AND TOPPING

2½ cups all-purpose flour

1 cup sugar

½ cup ground slivered almonds

1 teaspoon baking powder

¼ teaspoon salt

1 cup cold butter

1 egg

¼ teaspoon ground cinnamon

FILLING

4 cups fresh or frozen cranberries

1 cup sugar

Juice of ½ orange (4 teaspoons)

1 tablespoon cornstarch

1 teaspoon vanilla

1 Heat oven to 375°F. Grease bottom and sides of 13x9-inch pan with shortening or cooking spray.

2 In large bowl, mix flour, 1 cup sugar, the almonds, baking powder and salt. Cut in butter, using pastry blender or fork, until mixture looks like coarse crumbs. Stir in egg. Press 2½ cups of crumb mixture in bottom of pan. Stir cinnamon into remaining crumb mixture; set aside.

3 In medium bowl, stir filling ingredients. Spoon evenly over crust. Spoon reserved crumb mixture over filling.

4 Bake 45 to 55 minutes or until top is light golden brown. Cool completely in pan on cooling rack, about 1 hour. Refrigerate until chilled, about 2 hours. Cut into 6 rows by 4 rows. Store tightly covered in refrigerator.

1 Bar: Calories 210; Total Fat 9g (Saturated Fat 5g, Trans Fat 0g); Cholesterol 30mg; Sodium 105mg; Total Carbohydrate 30g (Dietary Fiber 1g); Protein 2g
Exchanges: 1 Starch, ½ Fruit, ½ Other Carbohydrate, 1½ Fat **Carbohydrate Choices:** 2

Sweet Success Stock up on cranberries while they're abundant in stores. Just toss them in the freezer and use as you need; they'll be good for about a year. If you're using frozen cranberries for this recipe, there is no need to thaw them first.

A food processor works well for grinding the almonds. You will need about ⅔ cup slivered almonds to measure ½ cup ground almonds.

Apricot-Cardamom Bars

32 bars | Prep Time: 45 Minutes | Start to Finish: 2 Hours 40 Minutes

FILLING

1	large orange
2	cups chopped dried apricots
¼	cup granulated sugar
⅔	cup water
2	tablespoons butter

COOKIE BASE

1	pouch (1 lb 1.5 oz) sugar cookie mix
1	teaspoon ground cardamom
½	cup cold butter
¼	teaspoon almond extract
1	egg, slightly beaten
½	cup sliced almonds, coarsely chopped

GLAZE

½	cup powdered sugar
2	tablespoons butter, melted
¼	teaspoon ground cardamom
¼	teaspoon almond extract
1	to 2 teaspoons warm water

1 Heat oven to 350°F. Spray bottom and sides of 13x9-inch pan with cooking spray.

2 Grate 2 teaspoons peel and squeeze juice from orange. In 2-quart saucepan, heat orange juice, orange peel, apricots, granulated sugar and ⅔ cup water to boiling over medium heat, stirring occasionally. Reduce heat to medium-low; simmer 15 minutes, stirring occasionally. Remove from heat. Add 2 tablespoons butter; stir until melted. Mash filling with fork or potato masher until fairly smooth. Set aside.

3 In large bowl, stir together cookie mix and 1 teaspoon cardamom. Cut in ½ cup butter, using pastry blender or fork, until mixture looks like coarse crumbs. Add almond extract and egg; toss with fork to combine. Reserve 1 cup crumb mixture. Press remaining crumb mixture in bottom of pan.

4 Bake 15 minutes. Spoon filling over warm cookie base. Stir almonds into reserved crumb mixture; sprinkle over filling. Bake 25 to 30 minutes or until topping is light golden brown. Cool 10 minutes.

5 In small bowl, stir glaze ingredients, using enough warm water until glaze is thin enough to drizzle. Spoon glaze into small resealable food-storage plastic bag; seal bag. Cut small tip off bottom corner of bag; squeeze bag to drizzle glaze over warm bars. Cool completely in pan on cooling rack, about 1 hour. Cut into 8 rows by 4 rows. Store covered at room temperature.

1 Bar: Calories 150; Total Fat 7g (Saturated Fat 3g, Trans Fat 0.5g); Cholesterol 20mg; Sodium 80mg; Total Carbohydrate 21g (Dietary Fiber 1g); Protein 1g **Exchanges:** 1½ Other Carbohydrate, 1½ Fat **Carbohydrate Choices:** 1½

Cinnamon-Cream Cheese Carrot Cake Bars

48 bars | Prep Time: 20 Minutes | Start to Finish: 1 Hour 45 Minutes

BARS

- 1 box (15.25 oz) carrot cake mix with pudding in the mix
- 1 cup butter, softened
- 2 eggs
- 3 tablespoons milk
- 1 teaspoon ground cinnamon
- ½ teaspoon maple flavor

FROSTING

- 1 package (8 oz) cream cheese, softened
- ¼ cup butter, softened
- 2 to 3 teaspoons milk
- 1 teaspoon vanilla
- ½ teaspoon ground cinnamon
- 4 cups powdered sugar

1. Heat oven to 350°F (325°F for dark or nonstick pan). Spray bottom and sides of 15x10x1-inch jelly roll pan with baking spray with flour.

2. In large bowl, beat bar ingredients with electric mixer on medium speed until well blended. Spread batter in pan.

3. Bake 19 to 24 minutes or until top is golden brown and toothpick inserted in center comes out clean. Cool completely in pan on cooling rack, about 1 hour.

4. In medium bowl, beat cream cheese, ¼ cup butter, 2 teaspoons of the milk, the vanilla and ½ teaspoon cinnamon with electric mixer on low speed until smooth. Gradually beat in powdered sugar, 1 cup at a time, until smooth and spreadable. Add remaining 1 teaspoon milk if needed. Frost bars. Cut into 8 rows by 6 rows. Store covered in refrigerator.

1 Bar: Calories 140; Total Fat 7g (Saturated Fat 4g, Trans Fat 0g); Cholesterol 25mg; Sodium 115mg; Total Carbohydrate 18g (Dietary Fiber 0g); Protein 1g **Exchanges:** 1 Other Carbohydrate, 1½ Fat **Carbohydrate Choices:** 1

The Wow Factor If you like, top these bars with raisins, sweetened shredded coconut and chopped nuts.

Gluten-Free Harvest Pumpkin-Spice Bars

49 bars | Prep Time: 15 Minutes | Start to Finish: 2 Hours 40 Minutes

BARS

- 1 box (15 oz) gluten-free yellow cake mix
- 1 can (15 oz) pumpkin (not pumpkin pie mix)
- ½ cup butter, softened
- ¼ cup water
- 2 teaspoons ground cinnamon
- ½ teaspoon ground ginger
- ¼ teaspoon ground cloves
- 3 eggs
- 1 cup raisins, if desired

FROSTING

- 1 container (16 oz) cream cheese creamy ready-to-spread frosting
- ¼ cup chopped walnuts, if desired

1 Heat oven to 350°F. Lightly grease bottom and sides of 15x10x1-inch jelly roll pan with shortening.

2 In large bowl, beat all bar ingredients except raisins with electric mixer on low speed 30 seconds, then on medium speed 2 minutes, scraping bowl occasionally. Stir in raisins. Spread batter in pan.

3 Bake 20 to 25 minutes or until light brown. Cool completely in pan on cooling rack, about 2 hours.

4 Frost bars with cream cheese frosting; sprinkle with walnuts. Cut into 7 rows by 7 rows. Store in refrigerator.

1 Bar: Calories 90; Total Fat 3.5g (Saturated Fat 1.5g, Trans Fat 0.5g); Cholesterol 20mg; Sodium 85mg; Total Carbohydrate 14g (Dietary Fiber 0g); Protein 0g **Exchanges:** ½ Starch, ½ Other Carbohydrate, ½ Fat **Carbohydrate Choices:** 1

Cooking Gluten Free? Always read labels to make sure each recipe ingredient is gluten free. Products and ingredient sources can change.

CHAPTER FOUR

Brownies

Praline Brownies

24 bars | Prep Time: 20 Minutes | Start to Finish: 2 Hours 40 Minutes

BROWNIES

1   box (1 lb 2.3 oz) fudge brownie mix

   Water, vegetable oil and eggs called for on brownie mix box

½   cup chopped pecans

FROSTING

½   cup whipping cream

6   tablespoons butter

1½   cups packed brown sugar

½   cup chopped pecans, toasted*

1½   cups powdered sugar

1   teaspoon vanilla

1   Heat oven to 350°F. Spray bottom only of 13x9-inch pan with cooking spray.

2   Make brownie mix as directed on box for fudge brownies, using water, oil and eggs. Stir in ½ cup pecans. Bake as directed on box. Cool completely in pan on cooling rack, about 1 hour.

3   In 2-quart saucepan, mix whipping cream, butter and brown sugar. Heat to boiling over medium heat, stirring frequently. Boil 1 minute, stirring constantly. Remove from heat. Stir in toasted pecans, powdered sugar and vanilla. Cool 5 minutes, stirring frequently.

4   Frost brownies. Let stand 30 to 45 minutes or until frosting is set. Cut into 6 rows by 4 rows.

*To toast pecans, spread in ungreased shallow pan. Bake uncovered at 350°F 6 to 10 minutes, stirring occasionally, until light brown.

1 Bar: Calories 280; Total Fat 13g (Saturated Fat 4g, Trans Fat 0g); Cholesterol 20mg; Sodium 105mg; Total Carbohydrate 41g (Dietary Fiber 0g); Protein 0g **Exchanges:** 2½ Other Carbohydrate, 2½ Fat **Carbohydrate Choices:** 3

Sweet Success Cut the brownies about 45 minutes after frosting them. The frosting will still be just slightly warm, which should minimize any cracks in the frosting.

Hazelnut-Mocha Brownies

24 bars | Prep Time: 20 Minutes | Start to Finish: 2 Hours 5 Minutes

BROWNIES

1	box (1 lb 2.3 oz) fudge brownie mix
¼	cup water
⅔	cup vegetable oil
2½	teaspoons instant espresso coffee powder or granules
2	eggs
1	cup chopped hazelnuts (filberts)

FROSTING

1	cup powdered sugar
½	cup hazelnut spread with cocoa
2	tablespoons butter, softened
2	to 3 tablespoons milk

1 Heat oven to 350°F. Grease bottom only of 13x9-inch pan with shortening or cooking spray.

2 In medium bowl, stir brownie mix, water, oil, espresso powder and eggs until well blended. Stir in hazelnuts. Spread batter in pan.

3 Bake 24 to 26 minutes or until toothpick inserted 2 inches from side of pan comes out clean or almost clean. Cool completely in pan on cooling rack, about 1 hour.

4 In medium bowl, beat powdered sugar, hazelnut spread, butter and 1 tablespoon milk with electric mixer on low speed until blended. Beat in additional milk, 1 tablespoon at a time, until desired spreading consistency. Frost brownies.

5 Let stand about 15 minutes or until frosting is set. Cut into 6 rows by 4 rows.

1 Bar: Calories 240; Total Fat 13g (Saturated Fat 2g, Trans Fat 0g); Cholesterol 20mg; Sodium 90mg; Total Carbohydrate 29g (Dietary Fiber 0g); Protein 1g **Exchanges:** ½ Starch, 1½ Other Carbohydrate, 2½ Fat **Carbohydrate Choices:** 2

The Wow Factor Love the lines on the frosting in the photo? Immediately after spreading the frosting, pull knife or metal spatula gently across frosting in diagonal, straight strokes.

Double-Espresso Brownies

50 bars | Prep Time: 25 Minutes | Start to Finish: 1 Hour 50 Minutes

BROWNIES

1½	cups all-purpose flour
1½	cups granulated sugar
4	teaspoons unsweetened baking cocoa
3	teaspoons instant espresso coffee powder or granules
½	cup water
¾	cup butter
¾	teaspoon baking soda
⅓	cup buttermilk
1	egg

FROSTING

¼	cup unsweetened baking cocoa
½	cup butter
⅓	cup buttermilk
4½	cups powdered sugar
1	teaspoon instant espresso coffee powder or granules
1	teaspoon vanilla

1 Heat oven to 375°F. Grease bottom and sides of 15x10x1-inch jelly roll pan with shortening or cooking spray. In large bowl, mix flour, granulated sugar, 4 teaspoons cocoa and 3 teaspoons espresso powder.

2 In 1-quart saucepan, heat water and ¾ cup butter to boiling. Pour over flour mixture; beat with spoon until smooth. Stir in baking soda, ⅓ cup buttermilk and the egg. Spread batter in pan.

3 Bake 18 to 23 minutes or until toothpick inserted in center comes out clean. Cool completely in pan on cooling rack, about 1 hour.

4 In 3-quart saucepan, heat ¼ cup cocoa, ½ cup butter and ⅓ cup buttermilk to boiling over medium heat, stirring frequently. Remove from heat. Stir in powdered sugar, 1 teaspoon espresso powder and the vanilla with whisk until smooth and spreadable. Frost brownies. Cut into 10 rows by 5 rows.

1 Bar: Calories 130; Total Fat 5g (Saturated Fat 2.5g, Trans Fat 0g); Cholesterol 15mg; Sodium 55mg; Total Carbohydrate 20g (Dietary Fiber 0g); Protein 0g **Exchanges:** 1 Starch, 1 Fat **Carbohydrate Choices:** 1

Crunchy Peanut Butter Brownies

24 bars | Prep Time: 20 Minutes | Start to Finish: 2 Hours

BROWNIES

1	box (1 lb 2.3 oz) fudge brownie mix
¼	cup water
⅔	cup vegetable oil
2	eggs
1	cup semisweet chocolate chips
15	peanut-shaped peanut butter–filled sandwich cookies, chopped

TOPPING

1⅔	cups peanut butter chips
¼	cup creamy peanut butter
½	cup chopped salted cocktail peanuts

1 Heat oven to 350°F. Grease bottom only of 13x9-inch pan with shortening or cooking spray.

2 In medium bowl, stir brownie mix, water, oil and eggs until well blended. Stir in chocolate chips and cookies. Spread batter in pan.

3 Bake 24 to 26 minutes or until toothpick inserted 2 inches from side of pan comes out clean or almost clean. Cool in pan on cooling rack 30 minutes.

4 In small microwavable bowl, microwave peanut butter chips and peanut butter uncovered on High 45 to 60 seconds, stirring every 15 seconds, until melted and smooth. Spread over brownies; sprinkle with peanuts.

5 Cover; refrigerate 40 minutes or until topping is set. Cut into 6 rows by 4 rows.

1 Bar: Calories 320; Total Fat 17g (Saturated Fat 4g, Trans Fat 0g); Cholesterol 20mg; Sodium 180mg; Total Carbohydrate 37g (Dietary Fiber 1g); Protein 4g **Exchanges:** 1 Starch, 1½ Other Carbohydrate, 3½ Fat **Carbohydrate Choices:** 2½

Sweet Success For added texture, substitute crunchy peanut butter for creamy.

Pretzel Brownies

32 bars | Prep Time: 25 Minutes | Start to Finish: 2 Hours 15 Minutes

CRUST

1½	cups crushed pretzels
¼	cup granulated sugar
½	cup butter, melted

BROWNIES

1	box (1 lb 2.3 oz) fudge brownie mix
¼	cup water
⅔	cup vegetable oil
2	eggs

FROSTING

1	cup powdered sugar
2	tablespoons butter, softened
2	squares (1 oz each) unsweetened chocolate, melted
1	teaspoon vanilla
2	to 3 tablespoons milk
½	cup crushed pretzels

1 Heat oven to 350°F. In medium bowl, mix crust ingredients. Press mixture in bottom of ungreased 13x9-inch pan. Bake 8 minutes. Cool 10 minutes.

2 In medium bowl, stir brownie mix, water, oil and eggs until blended. Carefully spread batter over partially baked crust.

3 Bake 24 to 26 minutes or until toothpick inserted 2 inches from side of pan comes out clean or almost clean. Cool completely in pan on cooling rack, about 1 hour.

4 In medium bowl, beat powdered sugar, 2 tablespoons butter, the melted chocolate and vanilla with electric mixer on low speed until combined. Beat in 1 tablespoon milk until blended. Beat in additional milk, 1 tablespoon at a time, until frosting is smooth and spreadable. Frost brownies. Sprinkle with ½ cup pretzels. Cut into 8 rows by 4 rows.

1 Bar: Calories 190; Total Fat 10g (Saturated Fat 3.5g, Trans Fat 0g); Cholesterol 25mg; Sodium 135mg; Total Carbohydrate 23g (Dietary Fiber 0g); Protein 1g **Exchanges:** ½ Starch, 1 Other Carbohydrate, 2 Fat **Carbohydrate Choices:** 1½

Sweet Success Use a food processor to easily crush pretzels.

One Step Further

Great Ideas for Brownies

A brownie is a brownie . . . or is it? Who can resist one of these decadent little bars of chocolate bliss? But don't stop there—take brownies to new heights with one step further. Start with homemade or brownies from a mix (that have been cooled completely) or even store-bought brownies.

Use whatever brownies you like; however, plain brownies (without pieces in them like nuts or chocolate chips) will work better for more intricate shapes. If the recipe you use has a frosting, skip it—leave the brownies unfrosted to try one of these ideas below or make up your own. Several of the ideas are also great ways to use leftover brownies (if you ever have leftovers)!

BROWNIE POPS

Cut brownies into rectangles or other shapes such as stars, hearts or Christmas trees. Insert a wooden craft or candy stick into one end of each brownie; place on tray or cookie sheet. Freeze uncovered 30 minutes. For about 15 brownie pops, microwave ⅔ cup semisweet chocolate chips and 1½ teaspoons shortening about 1 minute or until mixture can be stirred smooth. (If necessary, microwave an additional 5 seconds at a time.) Dip top third to half of each brownie in melted chocolate; scrape off excess with a spoon. Sprinkle with candy sprinkles; lay on waxed paper until chocolate has set.

BROWNIE ICE CREAM SANDWICHES

Place cut brownies on tray or cookie sheet; freeze 30 minutes. Top 1 brownie with any flavor of ice cream (slightly softened). Top with another brownie; gently press together. Roll edges in candy sprinkles, mini chocolate chips or crushed candy if desired. Freeze 30 minutes or until firm. Wrap each sandwich in plastic wrap; store in freezer.

BROWNIE FOOTBALLS

Cut brownies with football-shaped cookie cutter. Frost with desired chocolate frosting. Pipe on white decorator icing to look like footballs. You could also cut with other shaped cookie cutters—decorating the frosted brownies as desired with small candies, decorator icing or sprinkles.

CHOCOLATE-RASPBERRY BROWNIE FONDUE

Cut brownies into about 1¼-inch squares. Mix 1 container chocolate creamy ready-to-spread frosting and ⅓ cup raspberry preserves in microwavable bowl. Microwave about 20 seconds or until mixture can be stirred smooth. Pour into fondue pot; keep warm over low heat. Spear brownies with fondue forks and dunk into chocolate fondue. You can also dip marshmallows or bite-size pieces of fresh or dried fruit.

BROWNIE SHORTCAKES

Cut brownies into squares. Place 1 brownie on each serving plate; top with Sweetened Whipped Cream (page 109) and cut-up fresh fruit. Top with another brownie and repeat with additional whipped cream and fruit.

PEPPERMINT BROWNIE TORTE

Bake a pan of brownies in a 13x9-inch pan. Cut cooled brownies crosswise into 3 equal-size rectangles. Place 1 brownie rectangle on cake platter; spread with Sweetened Whipped Cream (page 109) and crushed peppermint candies. Top with another brownie rectangle, additional whipped cream and candies. Repeat with remaining brownie rectangle, whipped cream and candies. Cover and refrigerate until serving.

CHOCOLATE BROWNIE-TOFFEE SHOOTERS

Cut brownies with small circle-shaped cookie cutter or paring knife, so brownie circles will fit inside shot glasses. Layer brownies in shot glasses with pudding, toffee bits and Sweetened Whipped Cream (page 109), if you like. Cover and refrigerate until serving time.

PEANUT BUTTER–BROWNIE ICE CREAM SQUARES

Top a 13x9-inch pan of brownies with 1 to 2 pints each softened peanut butter and chocolate or vanilla ice cream. Sprinkle with salted cocktail peanuts. Drizzle with chocolate ice-cream topping. Cover and freeze about 5 hours or until firm. Place pan in refrigerator about 30 minutes before cutting to soften slightly.

Milk Chocolate–Malt Brownies

48 bars | Prep Time: 15 Minutes | Start to Finish: 1 Hour 50 Minutes

2 cups milk chocolate chips (about 12 oz)

½ cup butter

¾ cup sugar

1 teaspoon vanilla

3 eggs

1¾ cups all-purpose flour

½ cup chocolate-flavor malted milk powder

½ teaspoon baking powder

¼ teaspoon salt

1 cup chocolate-covered malted milk balls, coarsely chopped

1 Heat oven to 350°F. Grease bottom and sides of 13x9-inch pan with shortening or cooking spray.

2 In 3-quart saucepan, melt chocolate chips and butter over low heat, stirring frequently. Remove from heat; cool slightly.

3 Stir in sugar, vanilla and eggs. Stir in flour, malted milk powder, baking powder and salt. Spread batter in pan. Sprinkle with malted milk balls.

4 Bake 30 to 35 minutes or until toothpick inserted in center comes out clean. Cool completely in pan on cooling rack, about 1 hour. Cut into 8 rows by 6 rows.

1 Bar: Calories 100; Total Fat 4.5g (Saturated Fat 3g, Trans Fat 0g); Cholesterol 20mg; Sodium 55mg; Total Carbohydrate 13g (Dietary Fiber 0g); Protein 1g **Exchanges:** ½ Starch, ½ Other Carbohydrate, 1 Fat **Carbohydrate Choices:** 1

Sweet Success Be sure to only coarsely chop the malted milk balls so that you'll have pieces you can identify when biting into these lunchbox favorites.

Almond Macaroon Brownies

48 bars | Prep Time: 20 Minutes | Start to Finish: 2 Hours 5 Minutes

1 box (1 lb 6.25 oz) supreme brownie mix with pouch of chocolate-flavor syrup

Water, vegetable oil and eggs called for on brownie mix box

3 cups flaked coconut

1 cup slivered almonds, toasted*

1 can (14 oz) sweetened condensed milk (not evaporated)

¼ teaspoon almond extract

½ cup semisweet chocolate chips

½ teaspoon vegetable oil

1 Heat oven to 350°F. Spray bottom only of 13x9-inch pan with cooking spray.

2 Make brownie mix as directed on box for cakelike brownies, using water, oil and eggs. Spread batter in pan. Bake 28 to 30 minutes or until toothpick inserted 2 inches from side of pan comes out almost clean.

3 In large bowl, mix coconut, almonds, condensed milk and almond extract. Carefully spread mixture over baked brownies. Bake 15 minutes longer (filling will not brown). Cool completely in pan on cooling rack, about 1 hour.

4 In small microwavable bowl, microwave chocolate chips and oil uncovered on High 30 to 40 seconds, stirring every 10 seconds, until chips are softened and can be stirred smooth. Spoon melted chocolate into small resealable food-storage plastic bag; seal bag. Cut small tip off bottom corner of bag; squeeze bag to drizzle chocolate over brownies. Cut into 8 rows by 6 rows.

*To toast almonds, spread in ungreased shallow pan. Bake uncovered at 350°F 6 to 10 minutes, stirring occasionally, until light brown.

1 Bar: Calories 150; Total Fat 7g (Saturated Fat 3g, Trans Fat 0g); Cholesterol 10mg; Sodium 75mg; Total Carbohydrate 20g (Dietary Fiber 0g); Protein 2g **Exchanges:** ½ Starch, 1 Other Carbohydrate, 1½ Fat **Carbohydrate Choices:** 1

Football Field Brownies

24 bars | Prep Time: 25 Minutes | Start to Finish: 2 Hours 25 Minutes

1 box (1 lb 2.3 oz) fudge brownie mix

Water, vegetable oil and eggs called for on brownie mix box

6 craft sticks (flat wooden sticks with rounded ends)

White decorating icing (from 4.25-oz tube)

Green food color

1 container (12 oz) vanilla whipped ready-to-spread frosting

22 gummy bear candies (11 yellow, 11 red)

1 small (1 inch) chewy chocolate candy, unwrapped

1 Heat oven to 350°F. Line 13x9-inch pan with foil, leaving foil overhanging at 2 opposite sides of pan; spray foil with cooking spray.

2 Make and bake brownies as directed on box for 13x9-inch pan, using water, oil and eggs. Cool completely in pan on cooling rack, about 1 hour.

3 Meanwhile, make goalposts* using craft sticks and decorating icing. Use foil to lift brownies from pan; place on serving tray.

4 Add enough food color to frosting to achieve desired shade of green; stir well. Frost top and sides of brownies. Draw yard lines on frosting with white decorating icing. Place gummy bear candies on field for players.

5 Microwave chewy chocolate candy on High 3 to 5 seconds, just until moldable. Shape into football. Use decorating icing to draw laces on football. Place on field.

6 Insert goalpost at each end of field. Cut into 6 rows by 4 rows.

*To make goalposts: On tip of 1 craft stick, squeeze a dot of decorating icing. Center another stick on the dot of icing, forming a T. Break or cut a third stick in half. Squeeze a dot of decorating icing on the broken tip of each half and secure upright onto the ends of the stick that makes the top of the T. Repeat with remaining 3 craft sticks for second goalpost. Place on dry, flat surface until set, about 30 minutes.

1 Bar: Calories 160; Total Fat 7g (Saturated Fat 1.5g, Trans Fat 1g); Cholesterol 10mg; Sodium 60mg; Total Carbohydrate 22g (Dietary Fiber 0g); Protein 0g **Exchanges:** 1½ Other Carbohydrate, 1½ Fat **Carbohydrate Choices:** 1½

Sweet Success Use a plastic knife dipped in hot water to cut the brownies; this will help prevent them from sticking to the knife.

White Chocolate–Cherry Blondies

36 bars | Prep Time: 30 Minutes | Start to Finish: 2 Hours 10 Minutes

2 cups packed brown sugar

½ cup butter, softened

2 teaspoons vanilla

½ teaspoon almond extract

2 eggs

2 cups all-purpose flour

1 teaspoon baking powder

¼ teaspoon salt

12 oz white chocolate baking bars, cut into chunks

½ cup slivered almonds

½ cup chopped dried cherries

½ teaspoon vegetable oil

1 Heat oven to 325°F. Grease bottom and sides of 13x9-inch pan with shortening or cooking spray.

2 In large bowl, beat brown sugar, butter, vanilla, almond extract and eggs with electric mixer on medium speed until light and fluffy. On low speed, beat in flour, baking powder and salt until well blended.

3 Set aside ¼ cup of the white chocolate chunks. Stir remaining white chocolate chunks, the almonds and cherries into batter. Spread batter in pan.

4 Bake 35 to 40 minutes or until top is golden brown and set. Cool completely in pan on cooling rack, about 1 hour.

5 In small microwavable bowl, microwave reserved white chocolate chunks and the oil uncovered on High 30 to 60 seconds, stirring every 15 seconds, until melted; stir until smooth. Drizzle glaze over blondies. Let stand until set. Cut into 6 rows by 6 rows.

1 Bar: Calories 170; Total Fat 7g (Saturated Fat 3.5g, Trans Fat 0g); Cholesterol 20mg; Sodium 65mg; Total Carbohydrate 25g (Dietary Fiber 0g); Protein 2g **Exchanges:** ½ Starch, 1 Other Carbohydrate, 1½ Fat **Carbohydrate Choices:** 1½

Sweet Success The slivered almonds can be whole or chopped, or left out completely, if you like. And dried cranberries can be substituted for the cherries.

Macaroon-Topped Browned Butter Blondies

64 bars | Prep Time: 30 Minutes | Start to Finish: 3 Hours

BLONDIE LAYER

1½	cups butter*
2	pouches (1 lb 1.5 oz each) chocolate chip cookie mix
½	cup packed brown sugar
2	teaspoons vanilla
4	whole eggs
1½	cups dark chocolate chips

MACAROON LAYER

½	cup granulated sugar
2	tablespoons water
2	bags (7 oz each) sweetened shredded coconut
1½	cups unsweetened finely shredded coconut
4	oz (half of 8-oz package) cream cheese, softened
2	egg whites, slightly beaten

1 In 2-quart saucepan, melt butter over medium heat. Cook 8 to 11 minutes or until butter is light golden brown, stirring constantly. Remove from heat; cool completely, about 30 minutes.

2 Heat oven to 350°F. Line 13x9-inch pan with foil, leaving foil overhanging at 2 opposite sides of pan.

3 In large bowl, stir together cookie mixes, brown sugar, vanilla, whole eggs and cooled browned butter. Spread batter in pan.

4 Bake 25 to 30 minutes or until toothpick inserted in center comes out almost clean. Immediately sprinkle with chocolate chips; let stand 5 minutes. Spread melted chocolate over bars.

5 Meanwhile, in small microwavable bowl, mix granulated sugar and water. Microwave uncovered on High 30 to 60 seconds or until sugar is dissolved.

6 In large bowl, place sweetened and unsweetened coconut. Pour sugar mixture over coconut; beat with electric mixer on low speed until well mixed. Add cream cheese and egg whites; beat on low speed until blended. Spoon and gently press macaroon mixture onto partially baked blondie layer.

7 Bake 20 to 25 minutes or until light golden brown. Cool completely in pan on cooling rack, about 1 hour. Cut into 8 rows by 8 rows. Store lightly covered at room temperature up to 1 week.

*Do not use margarine or vegetable oil spreads.

1 Bar: Calories 200; Total Fat 12g (Saturated Fat 8g, Trans Fat 0g); Cholesterol 30mg; Sodium 125mg; Total Carbohydrate 21g (Dietary Fiber 1g); Protein 2g **Exchanges:** ½ Starch, 1 Other Carbohydrate, 2½ Fat **Carbohydrate Choices:** 1½

Sweet Success While most blondies are truly blonde, these scrumptious bars get their darker color from the browned butter. Be sure to cool the browned butter completely to prevent the chocolate chips from melting and turning your blondie into a brownie!

Butterscotch Blondies

48 bars | Prep Time: 15 Minutes | Start to Finish: 1 Hour 55 Minutes

½ cup plus 2 tablespoons unsalted butter*

2½ cups packed light brown sugar

2 cups all-purpose flour

2 teaspoons baking powder

½ teaspoon salt

¾ cup fat-free egg product

1 Heat oven to 350°F. Spray bottom and sides of 13x9-inch pan with cooking spray.

2 In 1-quart saucepan, heat butter over medium heat 6 minutes, stirring occasionally, until lightly browned. Pour into small bowl; cool 10 minutes.

3 Meanwhile, in large bowl, mix brown sugar, flour, baking powder and salt. Add egg product to browned butter; stir with whisk. Pour butter mixture over flour mixture; stir just until moistened. Spoon batter into pan; smooth top with spatula.

4 Bake 30 minutes or until toothpick inserted in center comes out clean. Cool completely in pan on cooling rack, about 1 hour. Cut into 8 rows by 6 rows.

*Do not use margarine or vegetable oil spreads.

1 Bar: Calories 90; Total Fat 2.5g (Saturated Fat 1.5g, Trans Fat 0g); Cholesterol 5mg; Sodium 55mg; Total Carbohydrate 15g (Dietary Fiber 0g); Protein 1g **Exchanges:** ½ Starch, ½ Other Carbohydrate, ½ Fat **Carbohydrate Choices:** 1

The Wow Factor Sandwich vanilla or chocolate ice cream between two of these blondies for a delicious, hand-held treat!

White Chocolate Chunk Blonde Brownies

36 bars | Prep Time: 20 Minutes | Start to Finish: 2 Hours

BROWNIES

2	cups packed brown sugar
½	cup butter, softened
2	teaspoons vanilla
½	teaspoon rum extract
2	eggs
2	cups all-purpose flour
1	teaspoon baking powder
¼	teaspoon salt
12	oz white chocolate baking bars, chopped
1	cup chopped walnuts

GLAZE

¼	cup semisweet chocolate chunks (from 12-oz bag)
1	teaspoon vegetable oil

1 Heat oven to 350°F. In large bowl, beat brown sugar, butter, vanilla, rum extract and eggs with electric mixer on medium speed until light and fluffy.

2 On low speed, beat in flour, baking powder and salt until well blended. Stir in white chocolate and walnuts. Spread batter in ungreased 13x9-inch pan.

3 Bake 25 to 35 minutes or until top is golden brown and set. Cool completely in pan on cooling rack, about 1 hour.

4 In small microwavable bowl, microwave glaze ingredients uncovered on High 30 to 60 seconds, stirring every 15 seconds, until melted; stir until smooth. Drizzle or spread glaze over brownies. Let stand until set. Cut into 6 rows by 6 rows.

1 Bar: Calories 180; Total Fat 9g (Saturated Fat 4g, Trans Fat 0g); Cholesterol 20mg; Sodium 65mg; Total Carbohydrate 24g (Dietary Fiber 0g); Protein 2g **Exchanges:** 1½ Other Carbohydrate, 2 Fat **Carbohydrate Choices:** 1½

Sweet Success You could use pecans instead of the walnuts, or you can make the brownies without the nuts, if you like.

Chocolate Chip Blonde Brownies

24 bars | Prep Time: 15 Minutes | Start to Finish: 1 Hour 45 Minutes

⅔ cup butter, softened

2 cups packed brown sugar

2 teaspoons vanilla

2 eggs

2 cups all-purpose flour

2 teaspoons baking powder

1 teaspoon salt

2 cups semisweet chocolate chips (about 12 oz)

1 Heat oven to 350°F. Spray bottom only of 13x9-inch pan with cooking spray.

2 In large bowl, beat butter, brown sugar, vanilla and eggs with electric mixer on medium-high speed until blended. On low speed, beat in flour, baking powder and salt until soft dough forms. Spread dough in pan. Sprinkle with chocolate chips.

3 Bake 25 to 30 minutes or until edges are golden brown. Cool completely in pan on cooling rack, about 1 hour. Cut into 6 rows by 4 rows.

1 Bar: Calories 240; Total Fat 10g (Saturated Fat 6g, Trans Fat 0g); Cholesterol 30mg; Sodium 190mg; Total Carbohydrate 35g (Dietary Fiber 1g); Protein 2g **Exchanges:** 1 Starch, 1½ Other Carbohydrate, 2 Fat **Carbohydrate Choices:** 2

The Wow Factor For an additional layer of flavor, sprinkle 1 cup sweetened flaked coconut over the bars immediately after removing from oven.

Blonde Brownies with Brown Sugar Frosting

36 bars | Prep Time: 25 Minutes | Start to Finish: 1 Hour 50 Minutes

BROWNIES

1	cup granulated sugar
½	cup packed brown sugar
½	cup butter, softened
1	teaspoon vanilla
2	eggs
1½	cups all-purpose flour
1	teaspoon baking powder
½	teaspoon salt

FROSTING

⅓	cup butter*
⅔	cup packed brown sugar
3	tablespoons milk
2	cups powdered sugar
½	teaspoon vanilla
½	cup chopped pecans, toasted if desired**

1 Heat oven to 350°F. In large bowl, beat granulated sugar, ½ cup brown sugar, ½ cup butter, 1 teaspoon vanilla and the eggs with electric mixer on medium speed, or mix with spoon, until light and fluffy. Stir in flour, baking powder and salt. Spread batter in ungreased 13x9-inch pan.

2 Bake 20 to 23 minutes or until golden brown and toothpick inserted in center comes out clean. Cool completely in pan on cooling rack, about 1 hour.

3 In 2-quart saucepan, melt ⅓ cup butter over low heat. Stir in ⅔ cup brown sugar; cook over low heat 2 minutes, stirring constantly. Stir in milk; cook until mixture comes to a rolling boil. Remove from heat.

4 Gradually stir in powdered sugar and ½ teaspoon vanilla, mixing well with spoon after each addition, until frosting is smooth and spreadable. If necessary, add more milk, a few drops at a time. Frost brownies; immediately sprinkle with pecans. Cut into 6 rows by 6 rows.

*Do not use margarine or vegetable oil spreads in the frosting.

**To toast pecans, spread in ungreased shallow pan. Bake uncovered at 350°F 6 to 10 minutes, stirring occasionally, until light brown.

1 Bar: Calories 150; Total Fat 6g (Saturated Fat 2.5g, Trans Fat 0g); Cholesterol 25mg; Sodium 80mg; Total Carbohydrate 23g (Dietary Fiber 0g); Protein 1g **Exchanges:** ½ Starch, 1 Other Carbohydrate, 1 Fat **Carbohydrate Choices:** 1½

CHAPTER FIVE

Slab Pies and Crostatas

Gooey Salted-Pecan Chocolate Slab Pie

16 servings | Prep Time: 35 Minutes | Start to Finish: 3 Hours 55 Minutes

PECANS AND PIE CRUST

2	cups pecan halves
1	box Pillsbury refrigerated pie crusts, softened as directed on box

CHOCOLATE COOKIE CRUST

1¼	cups all-purpose flour
¼	cup unsweetened baking cocoa
2	tablespoons sugar
¼	cup butter, softened

FILLING

4	eggs, beaten
1½	cups sugar
1½	cups light corn syrup
3	tablespoons butter, melted
1½	teaspoons vanilla
1	bar (3.5 to 4 oz) dark or bittersweet baking chocolate, cut into ½-inch pieces
1	to 1½ teaspoons coarse sea salt

SERVE-WITH, IF DESIRED

Vanilla ice cream or Sweetened Whipped Cream (page 109)

Chocolate curls

Additional pecan halves

1 Heat oven to 350°F. Place pecans in 13x9-inch pan. Bake uncovered 5 minutes, stirring occasionally, until light brown. Set aside.

2 Unroll pie crusts; place in 15x10x1-inch jelly roll pan. Press crusts in bottom and up sides as much as possible, overlapping about ½ inch in center. Use any additional crust, cut into ½-inch strips, to fill in spots on sides and in corners. Moisten seams with finger dipped in water, and press seams firmly to seal. Do not prick crust.

3 In medium bowl, mix flour, cocoa and 2 tablespoons sugar. Cut in ¼ cup butter, using pastry blender or fork, until butter is evenly distributed (mixture will be dry). Press firmly over unbaked crust in pan. Bake 15 minutes or until chocolate crust puffs slightly in center and forms a few cracks.

4 In large bowl, mix eggs, 1½ cups sugar, the corn syrup, melted butter and vanilla. Pour and spread filling over partially baked crust. Sprinkle with chocolate and toasted pecans.

5 Bake 15 minutes; sprinkle evenly with salt. Bake about 20 minutes longer or until filling is set. Cool completely in pan on cooling rack, about 2 hours 30 minutes.

6 Cut into 4 rows by 4 rows. If desired, cut each piece diagonally in half. Serve with ice cream; garnish with chocolate curls and additional pecans.

1 Serving: Calories 520; Total Fat 24g (Saturated Fat 8g, Trans Fat 0g); Cholesterol 65mg; Sodium 350mg; Total Carbohydrate 70g (Dietary Fiber 2g); Protein 5g **Exchanges:** ½ Starch, 4 Other Carbohydrate, ½ Very Lean Meat, 4½ Fat **Carbohydrate Choices:** 4½

Sweet Success Here's a twist on pecan pie, perfect for when you have a houseful to serve.

Apple Slab Pie

16 servings | Prep Time: 30 Minutes | Start to Finish: 2 Hours 25 Minutes

1 box Pillsbury refrigerated pie crusts, softened as directed on box

1 cup granulated sugar

3 tablespoons all-purpose flour

1 teaspoon ground cinnamon

¼ teaspoon ground nutmeg

¼ teaspoon salt

4½ teaspoons lemon juice

9 cups thinly sliced peeled apples (9 medium)

1 cup powdered sugar

2 tablespoons milk

1 Heat oven to 450°F. Unroll pie crusts; stack one on top of the other on lightly floured surface. Roll to 17x12-inch rectangle. Fit crust into 15x10x1-inch jelly roll pan, pressing into corners. Fold extra pastry crust under, even with edges of pan; seal edges.

2 In large bowl, mix granulated sugar, flour, cinnamon, nutmeg, salt and lemon juice. Add apples; toss to coat. Spoon into crust-lined pan.

3 Bake 33 to 38 minutes or until crust is golden brown and filling is bubbly. Cool on cooling rack 45 minutes.

4 In small bowl, mix powdered sugar and milk until well blended. Drizzle glaze over pie. Let stand until set, about 30 minutes. Cut into 4 rows by 4 rows.

1 Serving: Calories 220; Total Fat 6g (Saturated Fat 2.5g, Trans Fat 0g); Cholesterol 5mg; Sodium 170mg; Total Carbohydrate 41g (Dietary Fiber 1g); Protein 1g **Exchanges:** ½ Starch, ½ Fruit, 2 Other Carbohydrate, 1 Fat **Carbohydrate Choices:** 3

Sweet Success Mix 2 or 3 varieties of apples for the best taste and texture. Braeburn and Granny Smith are an unbeatable combination.

Apple-Pomegranate Slab Pie

16 servings | Prep Time: 45 Minutes | Start to Finish: 2 Hours 10 Minutes

CRUST

2 boxes Pillsbury refrigerated pie crusts, softened as directed on box

FILLING

12 cups thinly sliced peeled tart apples (about 4 lb)

1⅓ cups sugar

1 teaspoon ground cardamom or cinnamon

½ teaspoon salt

2 teaspoons grated orange peel

1 teaspoon vanilla

½ cup cornstarch

Juice of 2 oranges (about ½ cup)

1 cup pomegranate seeds

GLAZE

3 tablespoons whipping cream

2 tablespoons sugar

1 Heat oven to 400°F. On well-floured surface, roll 2 of the pie crusts together to 19x14-inch rectangle. Roll pastry onto rolling pin; unroll into 15x10x1-inch jelly roll pan. Press pastry in bottom and up sides of pan, allowing edges of pastry to overhang sides of pan.

2 In large bowl, toss apples, 1⅓ cups sugar, the cardamom, salt, orange peel and vanilla. In small bowl, mix cornstarch and orange juice. Add to fruit mixture; stir to combine. Spoon filling evenly into pastry-lined pan. Scatter pomegranate seeds over filling.

3 On well-floured surface, roll second pie crust to 17x12-inch rectangle. Place over filling. Fold top crust over bottom crust to seal, crimping edge slightly with fingers. With small knife, cut slits or decorative shapes in top crust. Brush top crust with whipping cream; sprinkle with 2 tablespoons sugar.

4 Bake 35 to 40 minutes or until crust is golden brown and juice begins to bubble through slits in crust. Cool on cooling rack at least 45 minutes. Cut into 4 rows by 4 rows. Serve warm or cool.

1 Serving: Calories 290; Total Fat 10g (Saturated Fat 3g, Trans Fat 0g); Cholesterol 0mg; Sodium 220mg; Total Carbohydrate 48g (Dietary Fiber 2g); Protein 2g **Exchanges:** ½ Starch, ½ Fruit, 2 Other Carbohydrate, 2 Fat **Carbohydrate Choices:** 3

Sweet Success You'll need 1 pomegranate to get 1 cup of seeds for this recipe. To remove seeds from a pomegranate, cut fruit in half and use a spoon to carefully lift seeds out; remove any white membrane from seeds. If a fresh pomegranate is not available, look for ready-to-eat pomegranate seeds (arils) in the produce department of the grocery store, or substitute sweetened dried cranberries in pomegranate juice.

Betty Crocker Sheet Pan Desserts

Caramel Apple-Ginger Crostata

6 servings | Prep Time: 20 Minutes | Start to Finish: 1 Hour 25 Minutes

1   Pillsbury refrigerated
    pie crust, softened as
    directed on box

6   cups thinly sliced peeled
    baking apples (6 medium)

½   cup packed brown sugar

3   tablespoons all-purpose flour

2   tablespoons finely chopped
    crystallized ginger

1   teaspoon ground cinnamon

1   tablespoon cold butter

1   tablespoon granulated sugar

⅓   cup caramel topping

1 Heat oven to 450°F. Line 15x10x1-inch jelly roll pan with cooking parchment paper. Unroll pie crust in pan.

2 In large bowl, toss apples, brown sugar, flour, ginger and cinnamon. Mound apple mixture in center of crust, leaving 2-inch border. Cut butter into small pieces; sprinkle over apples. Fold edge of crust over apples, pleating to fit. Brush crust edge with water; sprinkle with granulated sugar.

3 Loosely cover top and sides of crostata with foil; bake 20 minutes. Remove foil; bake 9 to 13 minutes longer or until crust is golden brown and apples are tender. Immediately run spatula or pancake turner under crust to loosen. Cool 30 minutes.

4 Cut crostata into wedges; drizzle with caramel topping.

1 Serving: Calories 380; Total Fat 10g (Saturated Fat 4.5g, Trans Fat 0g); Cholesterol 10mg; Sodium 260mg; Total Carbohydrate 70g (Dietary Fiber 2g); Protein 2g **Exchanges:** 1 Starch, ½ Fruit, 3 Other Carbohydrate, 2 Fat **Carbohydrate Choices:** 4½

Sweet Success Choose a crisp apple, such as Haralson, Honeycrisp or Braeburn, for this recipe.

Shop for crystallized ginger, usually packed in plastic containers, in the spice section or with other baking ingredients at the supermarket.

Cinnamon Apple Slab Pie

15 bars | Prep Time: 30 Minutes | Start to Finish: 5 Hours 30 Minutes

3   cups all-purpose flour

2   tablespoons sugar

¾   teaspoon salt

1¼   cups cold butter

10   tablespoons ice-cold water

1½   cups Cinnamon Toast Crunch™ cereal, crushed

8   cups sliced peeled tart apples (8 medium)

½   cup sugar

1   teaspoon ground cinnamon

1   egg, beaten

1 In medium bowl, mix flour, 2 tablespoons sugar and the salt. Cut in butter, using pastry blender or fork, until mixture looks like coarse crumbs. Sprinkle with water, 2 tablespoons at a time, stirring with fork until dough just comes together. Divide dough in half. Cover; refrigerate 2 hours.

2 Heat oven to 425°F. Spray bottom and sides of 15x10x1-inch jelly roll pan with cooking spray. Roll out half of the dough to 15x10-inch rectangle; place in pan. Sprinkle with cereal. In large bowl, toss apples, ½ cup sugar and the cinnamon. Arrange apples over cereal.

3 Roll out remaining half of dough to 15x12-inch rectangle. Cut lengthwise into ¾-inch-wide strips. Arrange strips diagonally in lattice design over filling; trim and seal edges. Brush with beaten egg.

4 Bake 15 minutes. Reduce oven temperature to 375°F. Bake 40 to 45 minutes longer or until crust is golden brown and apples are tender. Cool completely in pan on cooling rack, about 2 hours. Cut into 5 rows by 3 rows. Store loosely covered.

1 Serving: Calories 299; Total Fat 16g (Saturated Fat 10g, Trans Fat 0g); Cholesterol 0mg; Sodium 287mg; Total Carbohydrate 37g (Dietary Fiber 1g); Protein 3g
Exchanges: 1½ Starch, ½ Fruit, ½ Other Carbohydrate, 2½ Fat **Carbohydrate Choices:** 2½

Sweet Success Use a pizza cutter to cut your strips of pastry for the top crust. It's an easy way to make nice, even cuts.

Peach Slab Pie

16 servings | Prep Time: 30 Minutes | Start to Finish: 2 Hours 25 Minutes

1 box Pillsbury refrigerated pie crusts, softened as directed on box

¾ cup packed brown sugar

¼ cup cornstarch

2 tablespoons lemon juice

¼ teaspoon salt

9 cups sliced peeled peaches

1 roll (16.5 oz) refrigerated sugar cookies

1 Heat oven to 375°F. Unroll pie crusts; stack one on top of the other on lightly floured surface. Roll to 17x12-inch rectangle. Fit crust into 15x10x1-inch jelly roll pan, pressing into corners. Fold extra pastry under, even with edges of pan; seal edges.

2 In large bowl, mix brown sugar, cornstarch, lemon juice and salt. Add peaches; toss to coat. Spoon mixture into crust-lined pan.

3 Break cookie dough into coarse crumbs; sprinkle crumbs evenly over filling.

4 Bake 50 to 60 minutes or until crust is golden brown and filling is bubbling. Cool on cooling rack 45 minutes before serving. Cut into 4 rows by 4 rows.

1 Serving: Calories 310; Total Fat 11g (Saturated Fat 4g, Trans Fat 1.5g); Cholesterol 5mg; Sodium 260mg; Total Carbohydrate 50g (Dietary Fiber 1g); Protein 2g **Exchanges:** 1 Starch, ½ Fruit, 2 Other Carbohydrate, 2 Fat **Carbohydrate Choices:** 3

Sweet Success To save time, or if fresh peaches aren't available, substitute frozen sliced peaches, thawed and drained.

Amazing Crust Treatments

Slab pies are a great way to serve pie to a crowd. And they are the ultimate way to enjoy eating pie since it's the perfect ratio of crust to filling. Sweeten the pot by topping your slab pie with one of these dazzling crust treatments. Then keep quiet as the compliments pour in—no one needs to know just how easy they are!

Pre-Bake Treatments

Amp up the top crust with one of the following*:

SHINY CRUST Brush crust with milk.

SUGARY CRUST Brush crust lightly with water or milk; sprinkle with granulated or coarse sugar.

GLAZED CRUST Brush crust lightly with beaten egg or egg yolk mixed with a teaspoon of water.

Post-Bake Glaze

CITRUS-SCENTED GLAZE Mix ½ cup powdered sugar, 2 to 3 teaspoons milk, orange or lemon juice and 2 teaspoons grated orange or lemon peel in a small bowl. Brush or drizzle over warm baked pie crust.

Other Crust Treatments

STAR STRUCK Instead of topping your pie with the traditional top crust, use a cookie cutter (such as a star, flower or leaf) to cut shapes out of it. Sprinkle shapes with coarse sugar and arrange on top of pie, overlapping slightly as desired. (Brush with water for them to adhere to the crust.)

GIVE IT A GLAZE Mix 1 cup of powdered sugar and 1 tablespoon of milk in small bowl until smooth. Drizzle over baked slab pie with standard pastry crust. Let stand about 30 minutes to set before serving.

CUTTING-EDGE DESIGN Rather than just cutting small slits in the top crust, really make a statement! Cut slits creating a pattern on the top crust, making them wider and longer to let the filling peek through.

LOVELY LATTICE Cut strips of pastry from top crust, using a pizza cutter and a ruler to make even-width strips. Lay strips on a diagonal, equal distance apart. Turn pan and repeat on other side, laying strips in the opposite direction. Pinch ends of strips to bottom crust to seal; crimp edge if desired.

A HOLE BUNCH Before laying top crust on pie, cut out shapes from crust, using a small knife or cookie cutter. From small circles to hearts, the design is up to you. This works especially well with pies that have pretty-colored fillings, such as berry pies.

MESSAGE PIES Use 2-inch alphabet letter–shaped cookie cutters or a small paring knife to cut out letters from the top crust before placing on pie. Get creative! You can write "Happy Birthday" or "Happy Anniversary," or whatever message you like. You can use either the crust with the letter shapes removed or just the letter cutouts themselves.

*These treatments may make the pie brown more quickly. If this happens, lay a sheet of foil loosely over the top of the pie to slow the browning.

Raspberry-Almond Tart

24 servings | Prep Time: 15 Minutes | Start to Finish: 3 Hours 40 Minutes

CRUST

1   pouch (1 lb 1.5 oz) sugar cookie mix

½   cup cold butter

¾   cup chopped almonds

TOPPING AND GLAZE

1   package (8 oz) cream cheese, softened

⅓   cup sugar

6   cups fresh raspberries

⅓   cup red currant jelly

2   tablespoons honey

1 Heat oven to 350°F. Spray bottom and sides of 15x10x1-inch jelly roll pan with cooking spray.

2 Place cookie mix in large bowl. Cut in butter, using pastry blender or fork, until crumbly. Stir in almonds. Press dough in bottom and ½ inch up sides of pan.

3 Bake 20 to 25 minutes or until edges are light golden brown. Cool completely in pan on cooling rack, about 1 hour.

4 In small bowl, beat cream cheese and sugar with electric mixer on medium speed until well blended and smooth. Spread over cooled baked crust. Top with raspberries.

5 In small microwavable bowl, stir together jelly and honey. Microwave uncovered on High 20 to 30 seconds or until thin enough to glaze. Brush glaze over berries. Refrigerate 2 hours. Cut into 6 rows by 4 rows. Store covered in refrigerator.

1 Serving: Calories 220; Total Fat 11g (Saturated Fat 5g, Trans Fat 1g); Cholesterol 20mg; Sodium 120mg; Total Carbohydrate 29g (Dietary Fiber 2g); Protein 2g **Exchanges:** ½ Starch, 1½ Other Carbohydrate, 2 Fat **Carbohydrate Choices:** 2

Sweet Success Mascarpone cheese can be used in place of the cream cheese, and pecans can be substituted for the almonds.

French Peach Tart

12 servings | Prep Time: 30 Minutes | Start to Finish: 1 Hour 15 Minutes

2 tablespoons Original Bisquick mix

2 cups Original Bisquick mix

⅓ cup granulated sugar

⅓ cup butter, softened

1 egg

¾ cup whipping cream

⅓ cup sour cream

¼ cup powdered sugar

1 teaspoon vanilla

5 to 6 cups sliced peeled fresh or frozen (thawed) peaches

⅓ cup apple jelly, melted

1 Heat oven to 375°F. Spray cookie sheet with cooking spray; sprinkle with 2 tablespoons Bisquick mix.

2 In medium bowl, stir together 2 cups Bisquick mix and the granulated sugar. Cut in butter, using pastry blender or fork, until mixture looks like coarse crumbs. Stir in egg until soft dough forms. On cookie sheet, roll dough into 12x10-inch rectangle; pinch edges to form ½-inch rim.

3 Bake 8 to 10 minutes or until edges are golden brown. Cool 2 minutes. With large spatula, carefully remove crust to cooling rack; cool completely, about 30 minutes.

4 In chilled medium deep bowl, beat whipping cream, sour cream, powdered sugar and vanilla with electric mixer on medium speed 2 to 3 minutes or until stiff peaks form. Spread whipped cream mixture over crust. Arrange peach slices over whipped cream mixture. Brush with jelly. Serve immediately or refrigerate until serving. Cut into 3 rows by 4 rows. Store in refrigerator.

1 Serving: Calories 280; Total Fat 13g (Saturated Fat 7g, Trans Fat 0g); Cholesterol 50mg; Sodium 270mg; Total Carbohydrate 37g (Dietary Fiber 1g); Protein 3g **Exchanges:** 1 Starch, ½ Fruit, 1 Other Carbohydrate, 2½ Fat **Carbohydrate Choices:** 2½

Sweet Success To avoid cutting peach slices when cutting into serving pieces, cut the base into 16 rectangles after topping with the whipped cream mixture. Top each rectangle with peach slices.

Fresh Berry Slab Pie

16 servings | Prep Time: 20 Minutes | Start to Finish: 2 Hours 5 Minutes

1 box Pillsbury refrigerated pie crusts, softened as directed on box

2 containers (6 oz each) plain fat-free yogurt

6 oz (from 8-oz package) cream cheese, softened

3 cups sliced fresh strawberries

1½ cups fresh blueberries

1½ cups fresh raspberries

1 cup glaze for strawberries (from 13.5-oz container)

1 Heat oven to 450°F. Unroll pie crusts; stack one on top of the other on lightly floured surface. Roll to 17x12-inch rectangle. Fit crust into 15x10x1-inch jelly roll pan, pressing into corners. Fold extra crust under, even with edges of pan; crimp edges. Prick crust with fork.

2 Bake 10 to 12 minutes or until golden brown. Cool completely on cooling rack, about 30 minutes.

3 In medium bowl, beat yogurt and cream cheese with electric mixer on medium speed until smooth. Spoon into cooled baked crust. Refrigerate about 1 hour or until set.

4 In large bowl, toss berries with strawberry glaze. Spoon berry mixture over cream cheese layer. Store in refrigerator. Cut into 4 rows by 4 rows before serving.

1 Serving: Calories 200; Total Fat 10g (Saturated Fat 4.5g, Trans Fat 0g); Cholesterol 15mg; Sodium 210mg; Total Carbohydrate 25g (Dietary Fiber 1g); Protein 2g **Exchanges:** ½ Starch, ½ Other Carbohydrate, 2 Fat **Carbohydrate Choices:** 1½

Sweet Success This recipe works well with sliced peeled apples or peaches, too—substitute 6 cups of either fruit for all three types of berries.

Fresh Blueberry-Almond Tart

6 servings | Prep Time: 15 Minutes | Start to Finish: 45 Minutes

2 cups fresh blueberries

⅓ cup granulated sugar

4½ teaspoons cornstarch

2 tablespoons water

¼ teaspoon almond extract

1 Pillsbury refrigerated pie crust, softened as directed on box

½ cup sliced almonds

1 teaspoon white decorator sugar crystals

1 Heat oven to 400°F. In large bowl, mix blueberries, granulated sugar, cornstarch, water and almond extract.

2 Unroll pie crust on ungreased cookie sheet. Spread ¼ cup of the almonds over crust; press lightly into crust.

3 Spoon blueberry mixture onto center of crust to within 2 inches of edge of crust. Fold 2-inch edge of crust over filling, crimping crust slightly. Sprinkle crust edge with sugar crystals.

4 Bake 25 to 30 minutes, sprinkling remaining ¼ cup almonds over filling during last 5 minutes of baking, until crust is golden. Serve warm.

1 Serving: Calories 270; Total Fat 12g (Saturated Fat 3.5g, Trans Fat 0g); Cholesterol 0mg; Sodium 170mg; Total Carbohydrate 38g (Dietary Fiber 2g); Protein 3g **Exchanges:** 1 Starch, ½ Fruit, 1 Other Carbohydrate, 2½ Fat **Carbohydrate Choices:** 2½

Cherry-Pear Tart

8 servings | Prep Time: 20 Minutes | Start to Finish: 1 Hour

1 Pillsbury refrigerated pie crust, softened as directed on box

1 tablespoon cornstarch

2 tablespoons water

1 ripe large pear, peeled, thinly sliced (about 1 cup)

1 can (21 oz) cherry pie filling with more fruit

2 teaspoons grated orange peel

1 egg

1 teaspoon sugar

1 tablespoon sliced almonds, toasted*

1 Heat oven to 425°F. Line large cookie sheet with cooking parchment paper. Unroll pie crust on cookie sheet.

2 In medium bowl, stir together cornstarch and 1 tablespoon of the water. Stir in pear, pie filling and orange peel. Spoon filling onto center of crust to within 2 inches of edge. Carefully fold 2-inch edge of crust over filling, pleating crust slightly as necessary.

3 In small bowl, beat egg and remaining 1 tablespoon water; brush over edge of crust. Sprinkle with sugar.

4 Bake 20 to 25 minutes, sprinkling almonds over filling during last 5 minutes of baking, until crust is golden brown and pears are tender. Cool 15 minutes. Cut into wedges; serve warm. Store covered in refrigerator.

*To toast almonds, spread in ungreased shallow pan. Bake uncovered at 350°F 6 to 10 minutes, stirring occasionally, until light brown.

1 Serving: Calories 230; Total Fat 7g (Saturated Fat 3g, Trans Fat 0g); Cholesterol 30mg; Sodium 140mg; Total Carbohydrate 38g (Dietary Fiber 2g); Protein 2g **Exchanges:** 1 Starch, 1½ Other Carbohydrate, 1½ Fat **Carbohydrate Choices:** 2½

Sweet Success Choose a pear that is best for baking. Anjou, Bosc, French Butter or Seckel varieties all would work well.

Banana Split Tart

16 servings | Prep Time: 20 Minutes | Start to Finish: 1 Hour 15 Minutes

1   box Pillsbury refrigerated pie crusts, softened as directed on box

½   cup semisweet chocolate chips, melted*

2   containers (6 oz each) French vanilla yogurt

2   small bananas, sliced

1   can (21 oz) strawberry pie filling

1   cup fresh strawberries, sliced

1 Heat oven to 375°F. Remove pie crusts from pouches; unroll 1 crust flat in center of ungreased large cookie sheet. Place second crust flat over first crust, matching edges and pressing to seal. With rolling pin, roll out into 14-inch round.

2 Fold ½ inch of crust edge under, forming border; press to seal seam. If desired, flute edge. Prick crust generously with fork.

3 Bake 20 to 25 minutes or until golden brown. Cool completely, about 30 minutes.

4 Spread ¼ cup of the melted chocolate chips evenly over cooled baked crust. Spread yogurt over chocolate. Arrange banana slices on top of yogurt. Spread pie filling evenly over top. Arrange strawberries over pie filling. Drizzle remaining melted chocolate over top. Cut into wedges. Store in refrigerator.

*To melt chips, place in small microwavable bowl. Microwave on High 45 seconds; stir until smooth. If necessary, microwave an additional 15 seconds.

1 Serving: Calories 190 (Calories from Fat 70); Total Fat 8g (Saturated Fat 3.5g, Trans Fat 0g); Cholesterol 5mg; Sodium 140mg; Potassium 125mg; Total Carbohydrate 28g (Dietary Fiber 1g); Protein 2g **Exchanges:** ½ Starch, 1½ Other Carbohydrate, 1½ Fat **Carbohydrate Choices:** 2

Nectarine-Plum Crostata

8 servings | Prep Time: 40 Minutes | Start to Finish: 2 Hours 50 Minutes

CRUST

1½ cups all-purpose flour

1 teaspoon sugar

¼ teaspoon salt

½ cup cold butter

1 egg yolk

4 to 5 tablespoons cold water

FILLING

½ cup sugar

3 tablespoons all-purpose flour

¼ teaspoon ground cinnamon

3 cups sliced nectarines

2 cups sliced plums

1 tablespoon lemon juice

2 tablespoons cold butter

1 tablespoon sugar

1 In medium bowl, mix 1½ cups flour, 1 teaspoon sugar and the salt. Cut in ½ cup butter, using pastry blender or fork, until crumbly. Stir in egg yolk with fork. Sprinkle with water, 1 tablespoon at a time, tossing until ball of dough forms. Flatten ball to ½-inch thickness. Wrap in plastic wrap; refrigerate 30 minutes.

2 Heat oven to 425°F. On lightly floured surface, roll pastry into 13-inch round, about ⅛ inch thick. Place on ungreased large cookie sheet.

3 In large bowl, mix ½ cup sugar, 3 tablespoons flour and the cinnamon. Stir in nectarines and plums until coated. Sprinkle with lemon juice; stir gently. Spoon fruit mixture onto center of pastry, spreading to within 3 inches of edge. Cut 2 tablespoons butter into small pieces; sprinkle over filling. Fold edge of pastry up and over fruit mixture, pleating crust slightly as necessary. Brush edge of pastry with small amount of water; sprinkle with 1 tablespoon sugar.

4 Bake 30 to 40 minutes or until crust is golden brown and fruit is tender. Cool on cooling rack at least 1 hour. Store at room temperature up to 2 days, then store loosely covered in refrigerator up to 2 days longer.

1 Serving: Calories 340; Total Fat 15g (Saturated Fat 9g, Trans Fat 0.5g); Cholesterol 65mg; Sodium 180mg; Total Carbohydrate 45g (Dietary Fiber 2g); Protein 4g **Exchanges:** 1 Starch, 1 Fruit, 1 Other Carbohydrate, 3 Fat **Carbohydrate Choices:** 3

CHAPTER SIX

Candies

Salted Caramel-Pecan Pie Bark

35 pieces | Prep Time: 25 Minutes | Start to Finish: 1 Hour 45 Minutes

1 box Pillsbury refrigerated pie crusts, softened as directed on box

1½ cups coarsely chopped pecans

1 cup packed brown sugar

¼ cup water

1 teaspoon vanilla

½ cup salted caramel topping (from 11.5-oz jar)

½ cup semisweet chocolate chips

½ teaspoon coarse sea salt

1 Heat oven to 450°F. Line 15x10x1-inch jelly roll pan with cooking parchment paper, leaving paper overhanging at 2 opposite sides of pan.

2 Unroll pie crusts. Press crusts in bottom of pan, cutting to fit. Moisten seams with finger dipped in water, and press seams firmly to seal. Once bottom of pan is covered, use any additional crust, cut into ½-inch strips, along edges of pan to thicken edges (using same method as above). Do not prick crust. Bake 11 to 13 minutes or until golden brown.

3 Meanwhile, in 2-quart saucepan, heat pecans, brown sugar, water and vanilla to boiling over medium heat, stirring constantly. Boil 3 minutes, stirring constantly. Remove from heat. Immediately spread over hot crust. Drizzle caramel topping over pecan mixture.

4 Bake 3 to 5 minutes or until caramel is bubbly. Sprinkle with chocolate chips and salt. Cool in pan on cooling rack 30 minutes. Place pan uncovered in refrigerator about 30 minutes or until chocolate chips are set. Use parchment paper to lift bark from pan. Cut or break into 2-inch pieces.

1 Piece: Calories 130; Total Fat 7g (Saturated Fat 2g, Trans Fat 0g); Cholesterol 0mg; Sodium 110mg; Total Carbohydrate 17g (Dietary Fiber 0g); Protein 0g **Exchanges:** 1 Other Carbohydrate, 1½ Fat **Carbohydrate Choices:** 1

Sweet Success This is a unique and quick gift idea to make for a teacher or to take to a party as a hostess gift.

Peanut Butter-Chocolate-Toffee Crunch

40 pieces | Prep Time: 20 Minutes | Start to Finish: 1 Hour 35 Minutes

4½ cups Reese's™ Puffs™ cereal

1 cup butter

1 cup packed light brown sugar

½ teaspoon vanilla

2 cups semisweet chocolate chips (about 12 oz)

½ cup creamy peanut butter

2 cups miniature pretzel twists, coarsely chopped

½ cup salted peanuts

1 Heat oven to 350°F. Line 15x10x1-inch jelly roll pan with cooking parchment paper, leaving paper overhanging at 2 opposite sides of pan. Pour cereal in even layer in pan, clustering cereal tightly; set aside.

2 In 2-quart saucepan, melt butter over medium heat. Add brown sugar, stirring until well blended. Heat to boiling; cook about 5 minutes, stirring occasionally, until dark golden brown. Remove from heat; stir in vanilla. Drizzle over cereal; spread evenly with spatula.

3 Bake 10 minutes. Cool 3 minutes. Meanwhile, in medium microwavable bowl, microwave chocolate chips uncovered on High 1 minute, stirring every 15 seconds, until chips are softened and can be stirred smooth.

4 Stir peanut butter into melted chocolate until well blended. Drizzle over cereal; spread in even layer. Sprinkle with pretzels and peanuts; press into chocolate mixture.

5 Refrigerate about 1 hour or until chocolate is set. Use parchment paper to lift from pan. Cut into 5 rows by 4 rows; cut each piece diagonally in half.

1 Piece: Calories 170; Total Fat 10g (Saturated Fat 5g, Trans Fat 0g); Cholesterol 10mg; Sodium 130mg; Total Carbohydrate 17g (Dietary Fiber 1g); Protein 2g **Exchanges:** 1 Starch, 2 Fat **Carbohydrate Choices:** 1

Crispy Oatmeal Cookie Bark

24 pieces | Prep Time: 10 Minutes | Start to Finish: 1 Hour

¾ cup butter, melted

½ cup packed brown sugar

½ cup granulated sugar

1 teaspoon vanilla

1¼ cups all-purpose flour

½ teaspoon baking soda

½ teaspoon salt

¾ cup quick-cooking oats

¾ cup crisp rice cereal

Semisweet chocolate chips, melted, if desired

1. Heat oven to 350°F. Line cookie sheet with cooking parchment paper.

2. In large bowl, mix butter, brown sugar, granulated sugar and vanilla. Stir in flour, baking soda and salt. Gently stir in oats and cereal. On cookie sheet, press dough into 12x10-inch rectangle, about ¼ inch thick. (Dough will be crumbly at first.)

3. Bake 20 minutes or until firm and golden brown. Cool 10 minutes; remove to cooling rack with parchment paper still attached. Cool completely, about 20 minutes. Break bark into irregular pieces; dip in melted chocolate.

1 Piece: Calories 122; Total Fat 6g (Saturated Fat 4g, Trans Fat 0g); Cholesterol 0mg; Sodium 134mg; Total Carbohydrate 16g (Dietary Fiber 0g); Protein 1g **Exchanges:** ½ Starch, ½ Other Carbohydrate, 1 Fat **Carbohydrate Choices:** 1

Chocolate Butter Crunch Bark

36 pieces | Prep Time: 10 Minutes | Start to Finish: 40 Minutes

3¼ cups semisweet chocolate chips (about 19 oz)

½ cup finely chopped lightly salted dry-roasted peanuts

¼ cup creamy peanut butter

2 bars (2.1 oz each) chocolate-covered crispy peanut-buttery candy, chopped

1 Line cookie sheet with waxed paper. In medium microwavable bowl, microwave chocolate chips uncovered on High about 2 minutes, stirring once, until chips are softened and can be stirred smooth. Stir in peanuts and peanut butter.

2 On cookie sheet, spread chocolate mixture to ¼-inch thickness. Sprinkle chopped candy bars over top; press in lightly.

3 Refrigerate 30 minutes. Break into 2-inch pieces. Store between layers of waxed paper in airtight container at room temperature.

1 Piece: Calories 140; Total Fat 8g (Saturated Fat 4g, Trans Fat 0g); Cholesterol 0mg; Sodium 23mg; Total Carbohydrate 16g (Dietary Fiber 1g); Protein 3g **Exchanges:** 1 Other Carbohydrate, 1½ Fat **Carbohydrate Choices:** 1

Peppermint Bark

16 pieces | Prep Time: 10 Minutes | Start to Finish: 1 Hour 10 Minutes

1 package (16 oz) vanilla-flavored candy coating (almond bark), broken into pieces

24 hard peppermint candies

1 Line cookie sheet with waxed paper, foil or cooking parchment paper. Place candy coating in 8-cup microwavable measuring cup or 2-quart microwavable casserole. Microwave uncovered on High 2 to 3 minutes, stirring every 30 seconds, until almost melted. Stir until smooth.

2 Place candies in resealable freezer plastic bag; seal bag. Crush with rolling pin or flat side of meat mallet. Pour crushed candies into wire strainer. Shake strainer over melted coating until all of the tiniest candy pieces fall into coating; reserve the larger candy pieces.

3 Stir coating to mix evenly; spread on cookie sheet. Sprinkle with reserved candy pieces. Let stand about 1 hour or until cool and hardened. Break into pieces.

1 Piece: Calories 190; Total Fat 10g (Saturated Fat 8g, Trans Fat 0g); Cholesterol 0mg; Sodium 35mg; Total Carbohydrate 26g (Dietary Fiber 0g); Protein 0g **Exchanges:** 1½ Other Carbohydrate, 2 Fat **Carbohydrate Choices:** 2

Chocolate-Peppermint Bark Use chocolate-flavored candy coating instead of vanilla.

Drizzled Peppermint Bark In small microwavable bowl, microwave ½ cup semisweet chocolate chips or white vanilla baking chips and 1 teaspoon shortening uncovered on High about 30 seconds until chips are softened and can be stirred smooth. Drizzle over Peppermint Bark before letting stand 1 hour.

Apricot-Chai Almond Bark

24 pieces | Prep Time: 30 Minutes | Start to Finish: 1 Hour 55 Minutes

¾ cup slivered almonds

24 oz vanilla-flavored candy coating (almond bark), chopped

¼ cup apricot nectar

3 teaspoons ground cinnamon

1 teaspoon ground allspice

1 teaspoon ground cardamom

1 teaspoon vanilla

1 teaspoon grated lemon peel

¼ cup finely chopped dried apricots

1 Sprinkle almonds in ungreased skillet. Cook over medium heat 5 to 7 minutes, stirring frequently until nuts begin to brown, then stirring constantly until nuts are light brown. Cool 10 minutes. In food processor, process almonds until finely chopped; set aside.

2 Line 15x10x1-inch jelly roll pan with waxed paper. In medium microwavable bowl, microwave 12 oz of the candy coating on High 1 minute; stir. Microwave in 15-second intervals, stirring after each, until melted. Quickly stir in ⅓ cup of the chopped almonds. Spread evenly in pan. Refrigerate 15 minutes or until set.

3 In small bowl, mix apricot nectar, cinnamon, allspice, cardamom, vanilla and lemon peel; set aside. In medium microwavable bowl, microwave remaining 12 oz candy coating on High 1 minute; stir. Microwave in 15-second intervals, stirring after each, until melted. Quickly stir in apricot nectar mixture and dried apricots.

4 Pour and spread over chilled bark. Sprinkle with remaining chopped almonds. Refrigerate at least 1 hour. Break or cut into 2-inch pieces.

1 Piece: Calories 180; Total Fat 11g (Saturated Fat 6g, Trans Fat 0g); Cholesterol 5mg; Sodium 25mg; Total Carbohydrate 19g (Dietary Fiber 0g); Protein 2g **Exchanges:** 1½ Other Carbohydrate, 2 Fat **Carbohydrate Choices:** 1

Hosting a Bake Sale

Here's a fantastic way to raise money for a school, charitable organization or sick friend with overwhelming medical bills. A bake sale filled with great-smelling, eye-catching homemade treats is a great way to collect some cash. From breakfast treats to side-dish breads to desserts, everyone loves homemade goodies—who could resist purchasing from such a tempting display?

Getting Started

Enlist your family, friends, neighbors or coworkers into helping bake and run the sale.

- **SOLICIT BAKERS.** Post sign-up sheets, send emails or create an invite with free party-planning websites, asking for home-baked donations. Do they have a favorite family recipe that is always a hit? Have them make it!

- **FIND HELPERS.** Also include a sign-up, laying out specific tasks and times that people can sign up to help run the event. Consider asking for people to take a 2-hour shift—not so long that they won't commit and not so short that you can't fill all the slots.

- **ENGAGE THE COMMUNITY.** Contact local bakeries (including bakeries inside grocery stores) for donations.

- **GET THE WORD OUT.** Put up signs, send emails and post on social media when the event will be. Send a follow-up reminder so that people will remember to show up!

It's All In the Packaging

- Arrange for items to be dropped off the night before the sale.

- Host a wrapping party where all the goods are packaged to sell.

- Supply decorative paper plates, platters, food gift bags, cellophane and ribbon to wrap the goods. It's best if the food is wrapped in such a way that you can see what it is—people will be more likely to purchase it.

- Get crafty. Have a crafty friend? Ask them to design/make tags to attach to the wrapped items.

- Label each item with the name of the recipe on the tags. Feel free to get creative with the name—include at least the main flavor and what the item is (such as pie or bars) in the title. Make it fun and attention grabbing—sometimes that's all it takes to pique someone's interest.

- Price it right. Determine a few pre-set prices to choose from, for writing on the label or have the bake-sale be a free-will offering. You'd be surprised by how much someone will pay for a scrumptious treat!

It's Go Time

- **PICK A POPULAR SPOT.** Pick a high-traffic spot for the bake sale. Piggyback onto a school book fair or community craft show, or set up near the cafeteria at work—where lots of people will be passing by.

- **MAKE IT EYE-CATCHING.** Arrange the homemade goodies so they are easily visible. Use tiered cake platters, wrapping paper-covered boxes or other creative ways to add height, interest and visibility to the display. It's OK not to put everything out at once! Strive for a nice variety of types of baked goods, colors and shapes. Replenish as needed and move things to the front of the display area if they aren't selling quickly.

- **STASH THE CASH.** Have pens available for those who want to write checks and change for those purchasing with cash. Have a cash box for making change and holding the money or jars for free-will offerings.

- **BAG IT.** Offer bags with handles on hand for large purchases. Make it easy for them to buy—and buy a lot!

- **DONATE.** By bringing any unsold baked goods to your local food shelf, you can help your community a second time! Check with local food shelves in advance of the sale so that you will know where you can bring them.

Chocolate-Pecan Toffee

36 pieces | Prep Time: 30 Minutes | Start to Finish: 1 Hour 30 Minutes

1 cup sugar

1 cup butter or margarine

¼ cup water

½ cup semisweet chocolate chips

½ cup finely chopped pecans

1 In heavy 2-quart saucepan, heat sugar, butter and water to boiling, stirring constantly; reduce heat to medium. Cook about 13 minutes, stirring constantly, to 300°F on candy thermometer or until small amount of mixture dropped into cup of very cold water separates into hard, brittle threads. (Watch carefully so mixture does not burn.)

2 Immediately pour toffee onto ungreased large cookie sheet. If necessary, quickly spread mixture to ¼-inch thickness. Sprinkle with chocolate chips; let stand about 1 minute or until chips are completely softened. Spread softened chocolate evenly over toffee. Sprinkle with pecans.

3 Let stand at room temperature about 1 hour, or refrigerate if desired, until firm. Break into bite-size pieces. Store in airtight container.

1 Piece: Calories 90; Total Fat 7g (Saturated Fat 4g, Trans Fat 0g); Cholesterol 15mg; Sodium 35mg; Total Carbohydrate 7g (Dietary Fiber 0g); Protein 0g **Exchanges:** ½ Fruit, 1½ Fat **Carbohydrate Choices:** ½

Sweet Success When making toffee, a long spatula with a narrow metal blade is a good tool to have close by. You'll use it to both spread the toffee and the melted chocolate chips quickly and easily.

The Wow Factor For gift giving, fill decorative tins with toffee, separating layers with colored plastic wrap, colored tissue paper or waxed paper.

Layered Caramel-Chocolate Fudge

96 pieces | Prep Time: 30 Minutes | Start to Finish: 2 Hours 30 Minutes

CARAMEL FUDGE LAYER

2	cups packed dark brown sugar
¼	cup butter*
¾	cup evaporated milk (half of 12-oz can)
2	cups miniature marshmallows
2	cups white vanilla baking chips (about 12 oz)
1	teaspoon vanilla
1	cup chopped walnuts

CHOCOLATE FUDGE LAYER

2	cups granulated sugar
¼	cup butter*
¾	cup evaporated milk (remaining half of 12-oz can)
2	cups miniature marshmallows
2	cups semisweet chocolate chips (about 12 oz)
1	teaspoon vanilla
8	oz walnut halves or pieces (about 1½ cups)

1   Line 13x9-inch pan with foil, leaving foil overhanging at 2 opposite sides of pan; spray foil with cooking spray. In 3-quart saucepan, cook brown sugar, ¼ cup butter and ¾ cup evaporated milk over medium-high heat, stirring constantly, until sugar is dissolved. Heat to boiling, stirring constantly. Reduce heat to low; boil gently 5 minutes without stirring.

2   Remove from heat. Stir in 2 cups marshmallows, the vanilla chips and 1 teaspoon vanilla; stir until marshmallows and chips are melted and mixture is smooth. Stir in chopped walnuts. Quickly spread mixture in pan. Refrigerate 30 minutes.

3   In 3-quart saucepan, cook granulated sugar, ¼ cup butter and ¾ cup evaporated milk over medium-high heat, stirring constantly, until sugar is dissolved. Heat to boiling, stirring constantly. Reduce heat to low; boil gently 5 minutes without stirring.

4   Remove from heat. Stir in 2 cups marshmallows, the chocolate chips and 1 teaspoon vanilla; stir until marshmallows and chips are melted and mixture is smooth. Beat 30 seconds with spoon until glossy. Quickly spread mixture over caramel fudge layer. Sprinkle with walnut halves; press gently into fudge. Cover; refrigerate 1 hour 30 minutes.

5   Use foil to lift fudge from pan. Cut into 12 rows by 8 rows. Store tightly covered in refrigerator.

*Do not use margarine or vegetable oil spreads.

1 Piece: Calories 120; Total Fat 6g (Saturated Fat 2.5g, Trans Fat 0g); Cholesterol 0mg; Sodium 20mg; Total Carbohydrate 16g (Dietary Fiber 0g); Protein 1g **Exchanges:** 1 Other Carbohydrate, 1½ Fat **Carbohydrate Choices:** 1

Gluten-Free Double-Layer Mint Fudge

96 pieces | Prep Time: 15 Minutes | Start to Finish: 1 Hour 35 Minutes

FUDGE LAYER

- 2 cups semisweet chocolate chips (about 12 oz)
- 1 container (16 oz) chocolate creamy ready-to-spread frosting

PEPPERMINT LAYER

- 2 cups white vanilla baking chips (about 12 oz)
- 1 container (16 oz) vanilla creamy ready-to-spread frosting
- 2 drops red food color
- ½ cup finely crushed gluten-free peppermint candy
- 2 bars (1.55 oz each) milk chocolate candy, chopped

1 Line 13x9-inch pan with foil, leaving foil overhanging at 2 opposite sides of pan; lightly butter foil. In 3-quart saucepan, melt chocolate chips over low heat, stirring constantly, until smooth. Remove from heat. Stir in chocolate frosting. Spread in pan. Refrigerate 20 minutes.

2 Meanwhile, in another 3-quart saucepan, melt vanilla chips over low heat, stirring constantly, until smooth. Remove from heat. Stir in vanilla frosting and food color until well blended. Fold in crushed peppermint candy.

3 Carefully spread peppermint mixture over chilled chocolate layer. Sprinkle chopped candy bars over top; press in lightly. Refrigerate just until set, about 1 hour.

4 As soon as fudge is set, use foil to lift from pan. Cut into 12 rows by 8 rows. Store at room temperature.

1 Piece: Calories 90; Total Fat 3.5g (Saturated Fat 2g, Trans Fat 0g); Cholesterol 0mg; Sodium 35mg; Total Carbohydrate 13g (Dietary Fiber 0g); Protein 0g **Exchanges:** 1 Other Carbohydrate, ½ Fat **Carbohydrate Choices:** 1

Cooking Gluten Free? Always read labels to make sure each recipe ingredient is gluten free. Products and ingredient sources can change.

Extra-Nutty Peanut Brittle

60 pieces | Prep Time: 40 Minutes | Start to Finish: 1 Hour

½ cup light corn syrup

1 cup sugar

½ cup cold water

1 container (1 lb) cocktail peanuts (3 cups)

1 teaspoon vanilla

1 teaspoon baking soda

1 tablespoon butter*

1 Generously grease large cookie sheet and wooden spoon with butter. In 2-quart nonstick saucepan, heat corn syrup, sugar and water to boiling, stirring frequently. Boil 10 to 15 minutes, stirring frequently, until mixture reaches 230°F to 234°F on candy thermometer and forms a long thread when spoon is lifted and held above pan.

2 Stir in peanuts. Cook 10 to 15 minutes longer, stirring frequently, until peanuts turn golden brown and mixture reaches 300°F.

3 Meanwhile, in small bowl, stir vanilla and baking soda until soda is dissolved. Remove saucepan from heat; stir in vanilla mixture and 1 tablespoon butter. Quickly spread mixture on cookie sheet, smoothing top with back of buttered spoon to make a single layer of peanuts.

4 Cool about 20 minutes. Break into 1-inch pieces. Store in airtight container at room temperature up to 3 weeks.

*Do not use margarine or vegetable oil spreads.

1 Piece: Calories 70; Total Fat 4g (Saturated Fat 1g, Trans Fat 0g); Cholesterol 0mg; Sodium 50mg; Total Carbohydrate 7g (Dietary Fiber 0g); Protein 2g **Exchanges:** ½ Other Carbohydrate, ½ High-Fat Meat **Carbohydrate Choices:** ½

Crunchy Cinnamon-Toffee Candy

32 pieces | Prep Time: 15 Minutes | Start to Finish: 1 Hour 55 Minutes

4 cups Cinnamon Toast Crunch cereal

1 cup butter

1 cup packed brown sugar

2 cups semisweet chocolate chips (about 12 oz)

¾ cup chopped pecans or sliced almonds, toasted*

1 Heat oven to 350°F. Line 15x10x1-inch jelly roll pan with foil; spray foil with cooking spray. Spread cereal evenly in pan.

2 In 2-quart saucepan, heat butter and brown sugar, stirring with whisk, until butter is melted. Heat to boiling over medium-high heat, stirring occasionally. Reduce heat to medium; boil 2 minutes without stirring. Immediately pour mixture over cereal in pan.

3 Bake 12 minutes. Sprinkle chocolate chips on top. Let stand 5 minutes. Spread melted chocolate over top; sprinkle with nuts.

4 Cool completely in pan on cooling rack, about 1 hour. Refrigerate 20 minutes to set chocolate. Break into pieces. Store covered in refrigerator up to 1 week.

*To toast nuts, spread in ungreased shallow pan. Bake uncovered at 350°F 6 to 10 minutes, stirring occasionally, until light brown.

1 Piece: Calories 180; Total Fat 11g (Saturated Fat 6g, Trans Fat 0g); Cholesterol 15mg; Sodium 90mg; Total Carbohydrate 18g (Dietary Fiber 1g); Protein 1g **Exchanges:** ½ Starch, 1 Other Carbohydrate, 2 Fat **Carbohydrate Choices:** 1

Sweet Success For gift giving, fill decorative tins with candy, separating layers with colored plastic wrap, colored tissue paper or waxed paper.

Cashew Toffee

36 pieces | Prep Time: 30 Minutes | Start to Finish: 1 Hour

1   cup cashew halves and pieces
½   cup granulated sugar
½   packed brown sugar
1   cup butter or margarine
¼   cup water
½   cup white vanilla baking chips

1 Heat oven to 350°F. Line 15x10x1-inch jelly roll pan with foil. Spread cashews in pan. Bake 6 to 10 minutes, stirring occasionally, until light brown. Pour into small bowl; set aside. Set foil-lined pan aside.

2 In 2-quart heavy saucepan, cook granulated sugar, brown sugar, butter and water over medium-high heat 4 to 6 minutes, stirring constantly with wooden spoon, until mixture comes to a full boil. Boil 10 to 15 minutes, stirring constantly, to 300°F on candy thermometer or until small amount of mixture dropped into cup of very cold water separates into hard, brittle threads.

3 Stir in ½ cup of the cashews; immediately pour toffee into foil-lined pan. Quickly spread to ¼-inch thickness with rubber spatula. Sprinkle with baking chips. Let stand about 1 minute or until chips are completely softened. Spread softened chips evenly over toffee. Sprinkle with remaining ½ cup cashews.

4 Refrigerate about 30 minutes or until topping is firm. Break into 2x1-inch pieces. Store tightly covered at room temperature.

1 Serving: Calories 110; Total Fat 8g (Saturated Fat 4g, Trans Fat 0g); Cholesterol 15mg; Sodium 55mg; Total Carbohydrate 9g (Dietary Fiber 0g); Protein 1g **Exchanges:** ½ Fruit, 1½ Fat **Carbohydrate Choices:** ½

Sweet Success Use your favorite chocolate—dark, milk, semisweet— in this tasty toffee.

The Wow Factor For an extra-decadent dessert, sprinkle broken pieces of toffee over ice cream.

Metric Conversion Guide

VOLUME

U.S. Units	Canadian Metric	Australian Metric
¼ teaspoon	1 mL	1 ml
½ teaspoon	2 mL	2 ml
1 teaspoon	5 mL	5 ml
1 tablespoon	15 mL	20 ml
¼ cup	50 mL	60 ml
⅓ cup	75 mL	80 ml
½ cup	125 mL	125 ml
⅔ cup	150 mL	170 ml
¾ cup	175 mL	190 ml
1 cup	250 mL	250 ml
1 quart	1 liter	1 liter
1½ quarts	1.5 liters	1.5 liters
2 quarts	2 liters	2 liters
2½ quarts	2.5 liters	2.5 liters
3 quarts	3 liters	3 liters
4 quarts	4 liters	4 liters

WEIGHT

U.S. Units	Canadian Metric	Australian Metric
1 ounce	30 grams	30 grams
2 ounces	55 grams	60 grams
3 ounces	85 grams	90 grams
4 ounces (¼ pound)	115 grams	125 grams
8 ounces (½ pound)	225 grams	225 grams
16 ounces (1 pound)	455 grams	500 grams
1 pound	455 grams	0.5 kilogram

MEASUREMENTS

Inches	Centimeters
1	2.5
2	5.0
3	7.5
4	10.0
5	12.5
6	15.0
7	17.5
8	20.5
9	23.0
10	25.5
11	28.0
12	30.5
13	33.0

TEMPERATURES

Fahrenheit	Celsius
32°	0°
212°	100°
250°	120°
275°	140°
300°	150°
325°	160°
350°	180°
375°	190°
400°	200°
425°	220°
450°	230°
475°	240°
500°	260°

Note: The recipes in this cookbook have not been developed or tested using metric measures. When converting recipes to metric, some variations in quality may be noted.

Index

RECIPE TESTING AND CALCULATING NUTRITION INFORMATION

RECIPE TESTING:

- Large eggs and 2% milk were used unless otherwise indicated.

- Fat-free, low-fat, low-sodium or lite products were not used unless indicated.

- No nonstick cookware and bakeware were used unless otherwise indicated. No dark-colored, black or insulated bakeware was used.

- When a pan is specified, a metal pan was used; a baking dish or pie plate means ovenproof glass was used.

- An electric hand mixer was used for mixing only when mixer speeds are specified.

CALCULATING NUTRITION:

- The first ingredient was used wherever a choice is given, such as ⅓ cup sour cream or plain yogurt.

- The first amount was used wherever a range is given, such as 3- to 3½-pound whole chicken.

- The first serving number was used wherever a range is given, such as 4 to 6 servings.

- "If desired" ingredients were not included.

- Only the amount of a marinade or frying oil that is absorbed was included.